Publisher's Note

The present work is the final part of a trilogy written by John Metcalfe, of which the first and second volumes, *The Psalms of the Old Testament*, and *Spiritual Songs from the Gospels*, have already been published. These titles provide accurate metrical versions of passages from the psalms, the gospels and the New Testament epistles respectively, and are intended to be used together in the worship of God.

THE HYMNS
OF THE
NEW TESTAMENT

JOHN METCALFE

THE HYMNS

OF THE

NEW TESTAMENT

IN METRE

ACCORDING TO

THE AUTHORISED VERSION

IN THE UNITED STATES ALL
INQUIRIES...RESPECTING OUR
PUBLICATIONS MAY BE SENT TO:

PUBLISHING TRUST, U.S.A.
P.O. BOX 141281
GRAND RAPIDS, MI 49514-1281

JOHN METCALFE

THE PUBLISHING TRUST
Church Road, Tylers Green, Penn, Buckinghamshire.

Copyright Notice

© John Metcalfe Publishing Trust 1985

All rights reserved. No part of this publication may be reproduced, stored in a retrieval system, or transmitted, in any form or by any means, electronic, mechanical, photocopying, recording or otherwise, without the permission of the John Metcalfe Publishing Trust, Church Road, Tylers Green, Penn, Buckinghamshire, U.K.

—

Printed and Published by
The Publishing Trust
Church Road, Tylers Green
Penn, Buckinghamshire

—

First published September 1985

—

ISBN 0 9506366 9 X

—

Recommended Price £2.50

—

Contents

Author's Note	i
The Hymns of the New Testament	iii
The Hymns (1-219)	1
Index of First Lines	233
Selected Verses for Singing	241
Textual Index	253
Sources of Recommended Tunes	265

THE PSALMS AND HYMNS AND SPIRITUAL SONGS

author's note

The LORD is he through whom this work began, and had it not been sustained by him throughout, surely no conclusion would have been reached. This is as true of the constant revisions, year after year, of the interminable typing, composing and paginating, as it is of the provision of so much equipment, and of the new-found skills required to produce work of the quality evident in the highly-subsidised end-product. 'This is the LORD's doing, and it is marvellous in our eyes.'

Although my name appears as the author, this work is the result of being equally yoked together with true brethren, spiritual yokefellows, and fellow-labourers in Christ Jesus. The saints met at Bethlehem Meeting Hall in Tylers Green, with their prayers, their devotion, and their self-sacrifice in Christ Jesus our Lord, are those to whom the singers owe a great debt of love in the service of God.

Nevertheless our voice is one, as is our desire: to say to every singer, Give glory to God alone, through Jesus Christ our Lord. Amen.

JOHN METCALFE

THE HYMNS OF THE NEW TESTAMENT

The publication firstly of THE PSALMS OF THE OLD TESTAMENT, followed by the SPIRITUAL SONGS FROM THE GOSPELS, has its conclusion in the present work, THE HYMNS OF THE NEW TESTAMENT. This completes the threefold 'psalms and hymns and spiritual songs', the last volume providing hymns from the book of Acts through to that of Revelation.

In these hymns the very words of the New Testament are set into simple common-metre verse with as little alteration as possible, so that the singer may feel that it is the scripture itself that is being sung.

Although change has been unavoidable, nevertheless it has been executed with the utmost care, using equivalent words faithful to the original, and consistent with text and context. No doctrinal words, no essential truths, no divine names, have been altered or omitted in any case.

This must be very near to what the apostles meant by 'hymns' in the New Testament, and to what was actually sung by the church in the beginning.

What has been handed down to us from the subsequent historical churches, the various denominations, and by modern evangelicalism, is clearly very, very far short of this, even at its best. The plain truth is, we have had nothing like it at all. And the inevitable result has been that in both spirit and truth our singing is impoverished

THE HYMNS OF THE NEW TESTAMENT

and limited, and has suffered far more than we know in consequence.

This becomes obvious from what has been allowed to evolve at the present time. The renaissance of sacramental hymns, lauding the real presence in the mass, or as they now prefer to call it, the eucharist, speaks for itself. Taken together with the development of the depraved and real evil of 'beat' music, swiftly commercialised as 'Christian group entertainment', with its 'stars' and 'folk-idols', why, this is nothing other than 'the people sat down to eat and drink, and rose up to play,' I Corinthians 10:7.

Had our hymns and songs been what they should have been, the sheer tone of our spiritual singing would have been an insurmountable barrier against all this.

An honest examination of the various hymn-books will reveal the sober truth that none agrees with the order of the New Testament, or of its books, in the arrangement of hymns. Some of the hymn-book sections cut right across both the letter and the spirit of the word of God. Conversely, the range of the doctrine of Christ in its fulness will be looked for in vain in these various compositions.

As to the hymns themselves, the briefest and most charitable examination will bring the swift discovery that many are at total variance with both the doctrine and experience of the new testament, and that they substitute human sentiment for experimental Christianity.

Yet regarding the praise of God, the one and the only question that should concern the real Christian is this: What is a hymn within the apostolic meaning of the word, and what comprises the hymn-book?

The answer is both certain and sure. That alone is a hymn which fully agrees with the doctrine of Christ and of

THE HYMNS OF THE NEW TESTAMENT

his holy apostles, and which expresses in verse form the very words of scripture. Anything else composed by man is by so much a departure. Consequently the hymn-book, in the sum of those hymns of which it is composed, should answer to the whole range of divinely revealed doctrine and experience, and nothing else.

In a word, the hymn-book must cover the whole New Testament. This is precisely what THE HYMNS OF THE NEW TESTAMENT, together with the SPIRITUAL SONGS FROM THE GOSPELS, has achieved, and achieved for the first time.

Now this—or its equivalent—should have been handed down to us, and nothing else should have been handed down to us. The harm that has been perpetuated from age to age by the repetition of venerated human compositions is incalculable. Conversely, the good that should have accrued from the singing of the word of God would have been beyond measure. Indeed, according to the apostle, not otherwise might 'the word of Christ dwell in you richly in all wisdom', in consequence of which you would be enabled to 'speak to yourselves in psalms and hymns and spiritual songs, singing and making melody in your heart to the Lord.' And without which such speech in melody is utterly impossible.

As to the title 'THE HYMNS OF THE NEW TESTAMENT' being applied to the epistles, I do not say that no spiritual songs occur in this part of the scripture. Just as I cannot say that no hymns occur in the four gospels. But it has seemed appropriate to me to name the present volume in this particular way, as encompassing the hymns of the church in the New Testament, and, if so, the books from Acts to Revelation.

But this is of little importance. What really matters is that we sing the very word of Christ, not the word of sentimental and undisciplined poets; that we hymn the

THE HYMNS OF THE NEW TESTAMENT

inspired word of God, and not the word of fallible man; that we go back to the holy scripture, and do not follow the harmful and lawless traditions perpetuated by an apostate and fallen Christendom.

It is as true in singing as in all divine service, that nothing can be regarded as acceptable worship but what is wholly agreeable to the word of God. Equally, nothing can really edify the spiritual, except that it conforms to the word of Christ. Moreover, nothing can establish the soul, save that the Spirit of truth witnesses to the conscience in perfect harmony with the holy scriptures.

And, assuredly, to harmonise with such a witness is a wonderful and immeasurable blessing. It is at one and the same time to worship God and the Father, to glorify the Lord Jesus Christ, to honour the Holy Ghost, to conform to the word of God, to obey the gospel, to admonish one another, and to sing with melody in our hearts to the Lord. Only thus can we say,

> 'I will sing with the spirit,
> and I will sing with the understanding also.'
>
> *I Corinthians 14:15*

In view of this, and the performance of the same by faith continually, may the Lord greatly bless both the singer and the singing thereof, for his name's sake and praise. Amen.

★

THE HYMNS OF THE NEW TESTAMENT

> 'And now
> shall mine head be lifted up
> above mine enemies round about me:
> therefore will I offer in his tabernacle
> sacrifices of joy;
> I will sing,
> yea, I will sing praises
> unto the LORD.'
>
> *Psalm 27:6*

JOHN METCALFE

THE HYMNS

Hymn 1

Acts 1:1-4

S. Magnus

1 THE former treatise hath been made
    of all that Jesus wrought,
  throughout the gospel setting forth
    that which he did and taught,

2 Till he that day was taken up,
    when given first had he
  charge through the Holy Ghost to those
    that his apostles be:

3 To whom he showed himself alive,
    when he from death was raised,
  by many proofs infallible,
    seen of them forty days;

4 And speaking of that which unto
    God's kingdom doth pertain:
  and, being with them met, he them
    commanded to remain,

5 Nor yet to leave Jerusalem,
    but there abide, saith he,
  and for the Father's promise wait,
    which ye have heard of me.

Hymn 2

Acts 1:5, 8-11

Colchester

1 WITH water truly John baptised,
    said Jesus, but I you
  baptise shall with the Holy Ghost
    ere many days ensue.

2 And when the Holy Ghost is come
    upon you from on high
  then pow'r ye shall receive, and ye
    of me shall testify,

3 Both in Jerus'lem, and the coasts
    about Judaea round,
  proceeding through Samaria,
    unto earth's utmost bound.

4 And when he spoken had these things,
    whilst him behold did they,
  he went up from them in a cloud,
    and taken was away.

5 And whilst they into heaven looked,
    as he went from their sight,
  behold, two men did by them stand
    in shining raiment white:

6 Which also unto them did say,
    Ye men of Galilee,
  why into heaven gazing up,
    still standing here are ye?

ACTS

7 For this same Jesus, taken up
     to heaven, even so
  shall in like manner come again
     as ye have seen him go.

Hymn 3

Acts 2:1-4,(6,11,14)16-17

Dunfermline

1 NOW when the feast of Pentecost
     was reckoned to the day,
  together gathered in one place
     with one accord were they;

2 And suddenly from heaven came
     a rushing mighty sound
  as of a wind that filled the house
     where sitting they were found.

3 And cloven tongues like as of fire
     unto them did appear,
  and, lo, the same was seen to sit
     upon each of them there.

4 And with the Holy Ghost they all
     were filled, and so began
  to speak with other tongues, as speech
     the Spirit gave each man.

5 And all the multitude them heard
     each one in his own tongue,
  as they declared the wondrous works
     and marvels God had done.

6 And forth with the eleven then
    stood Peter, and said he,
This which ye hear is that which Joel
    the prophet did foresee;

7 And it shall come to pass, as nigh
    the latter days shall draw,
that of my Spirit I, saith God,
    upon all flesh will pour.

Hymn 4
Acts 2:37-47

Petersham

1 AS Peter to the people spake,
    pricked in their heart were they.
What, men and brethren, shall we do?
    they unto him did say.

2 Then Peter unto them replied,
    Repent each one do ye,
and in the name of Jesus Christ
    baptised with water be,

3 That be remitted may your sins;
    and so ye shall receive
the Holy Ghost which given is
    to them that do believe.

4 For unto you the promise is,
    and to your children all,
and those far off, as many as
    the Lord our God shall call.

ACTS

5 And Peter many other words
   in testimony gave,
   exhorting from this age perverse
   that they themselves should save.

6 And they baptised were that received
   his word with gladness then:
   and to them added were that day
   about three thousand men.

7 In the apostles' doctrine they
   continued steadfastly,
   in fellowship, and breaking bread,
   and prayers continually.

8 And fear and trembling came upon
   the soul of every one:
   and many signs and wonders were
   by the apostles done.

9 And all believers shared all things,
   and were in heart agreed,
   and sold their goods, and parted them,
   as every man had need.

10 And in the temple worshipping
    continually were they,
    in unity with one accord
    assembling every day:

11 And breaking bread from house to house,
    they ate their meat as one
    with joy and singleness of heart,
    in praise to God alone;

12 And all the people favoured them.
      And so continually
    each day the Lord did to the church
      add such as saved should be.

Hymn 5

Acts 4:10-13

Ellacombe

1 TO you, and Isr'el all, be known
      the truth which we proclaim:
    by Jesus Christ of Nazareth,
      and by his holy name,

2 Whom ye did crucify, whom God
      raised up with mighty hand,
    by him it is that this man here
      before you whole doth stand.

3 This is the stone which ye that build
      in scorn aside have laid,
    but which is chosen, and is now
      head of the corner made.

4 Salvation in none other is:
      'neath heaven verily
    there is none other name 'mong men
      whereby we saved must be.

5 Now when of Peter and of John
      the boldness they did see,
    and men unlearn'd and ignorant
      perceiving them to be:

ACTS

6 They marvelled, and took knowledge that
     they had with Jesus been,
   and could say nothing 'gainst the things
     by all the people seen.

Hymn 6

Acts 5:11-16

Winchester

1 UPON the church there came great fear,
       with those that heard each one;
   and by the twelve apostles' hands
     were many wonders done.

2 (Unto the porch of Solomon
     with one accord they came,
   and of the rest there durst no man
     himself join to the same.

3 But them the people magnified:
     and multitudes believed
   of men and women, whom the Lord
     unto himself received.)

4 Yea, insomuch that in the streets
     the sick they down did lie
   on beds and couches everywhere
     that Peter should pass by;

5 If at the least in passing he
     might overshadow some.
   Then from the cities round about
     a multitude did come:

HYMNS OF THE NEW TESTAMENT

6 And to Jerusalem they brought
    the sick on beds that lay,
  and those by unclean spirits vexed:
    and healed each one were they.

Hymn 7
Acts 5:29-33

Abney

1 WITH Peter the apostles stood,
      and to the Jews did say,
  Than give place unto men we ought
      God rather to obey.

2 Our fathers' God raised Jesus up,
      whom ye hanged on a tree.
  Yea, God with his right hand hath him
      exalted made to be;

3 A Prince he is, a Saviour great,
      repentance for to give
  to Israel, that all their sins
      he freely might forgive.

4 And with the Holy Ghost are we
      his witnesses this day,
  whom God hath given unto them
      that him in truth obey.

5 When they heard that, then to the heart
      convicted were they all,
  and that they might them put to death
      they did for counsel call.

Hymn 8
Acts 20:25-31

Abbey

1 I KNOW that all of you, said Paul,
....among whom heretofore
I have God's kingdom preaching gone,
....shall see my face no more.

2 Wherefore I you to record take,
....and to you testify,
that from the blood of every man
....found pure this day am I.

3 God's counsel all I have not shunned
....unto you to declare.
Do ye now therefore of yourselves
....and all the flock take care;

4 Which by the Holy Ghost ye have
....been called to oversee,
to feed the church of God, which bought
....with his own blood hath he.

5 For this I know, that grievous wolves
....among you enter shall,
which will, soon after I depart,
....not spare the flock at all.

6 Yea, and of your own selves shall men
....rise up, that so they may
perverse things speak, and after them
....disciples draw away.

9

HYMNS OF THE NEW TESTAMENT

7 Watch therefore, and recall, that by
    the space of three full years
I did not cease to warn each one
    both night and day with tears.

HYMN 9
Acts 26:13-18

Glasgow

1 AT noon, said Paul, I in the way
    from heaven saw a light
above the brightness of the sun,
    about me shining bright;

2 They, too, which journeyed with me saw:
    and when we all did fall
upon the earth, I heard a voice
    in Hebrew cry, Saul, Saul,

3 Why dost thou persecute me so?
    to kick 'tis hard for thee
against the pricks. Then said I, Lord,
    who art thou? And said he,

4 I Jesus am, and it is I
    whom persecute dost thou.
But rise, and stand upon thy feet:
    appear I to thee now

5 E'en for this purpose, that thee make
    a minister might I,
that of these things which thou hast seen
    thou mightest testify,

ROMANS

6 And of those which I will thee show;
    henceforth deliv'ring thee
from people, and the Gentiles all,
    to whom thou sent shalt be;

7 Their eyes to open, them to turn
    from darkness unto light,
that from the pow'r of Satan's wrath
    be turned to God they might;

8 That through remission of their sins
    they might forgiven be,
and heirs be 'mong the sanctified
    by faith that is in me.

Hymn 10

Romans 2:5-9

Dalehurst

1 IN that day when revealed shall be
    the righteous wrath of God,
then he, according to their deeds,
    will justly men reward.

2 Those that in doing what is good,
    by patience constantly,
do seek for glory, honour true,
    and immortality,

3 At last shall reap eternal life.
    Contrariwise all they
that are contentious, and in heart
    do not the truth obey,

4 But who obey unrighteousness
    shall indignation reap,
  yea, wrath and tribulation mixed
    with anguish sore and deep.

Hymn 11
Romans 3:19-26

Noel

1 NOW know we that whatever things
    the law to men doth say,
  it saith to those found under law,
    that they should it obey:

2 That every mouth may by the law
    be silenced and made dumb,
  and that before God all the world
    guiltworthy may become.

3 For by deeds of the law no flesh
    shall in his sight endure
  as justified: because of sin
    the knowledge is by law.

4 But now the righteousness of God
    without the law is shown,
  by law and prophets having been
    both witnessed and foreknown;

5 That righteousness of God by faith
    of Jesus Christ withal,
  which unto all is that believe,
    yea, and upon them all:

ROMANS

6 For 'twixt them there no difference is:
      for sin they all have wrought,
   and likewise of God's glory great
      hath every one come short;

7 As being freely justified
      by grace and favour his,
   through the redemption wrought by him
      that in Christ Jesus is:

8 Whom a propitiation true
      God hath set forth on high
   through that belief which in his blood
      assuredly doth lie:

9 Thus to declare his righteousness
      according to his mind,
   for sins' remission that are past,
      through God's forbearance kind;

10 Yea, to declare his righteousness,
      that so he might be just,
   and justifier be of him
      that doth in Jesus trust.

Hymn 12

Romans 3:27-31

Hebdomadal

1 WHERE then is boasting? If it be
      excluded, by what law?
   of works? Nay, but the law of faith,
      which stablished is and sure.

2 Conclude we therefore that a man
     is freely justified
  by faith without the deeds of which
     the law hath testified.

3 Is he God of the Jews alone?
     or of the Gentiles too?
  Yes, of the Gentiles also, for
     them likewise he foreknew;

4 One God, the circumcision which
     by faith shall justify,
  and the uncircumcision too,
     through faith that bringeth nigh.

5 Do we make void the law through faith,
     that it annulled should be?
  Nay, God forbid, for by the truth
     the law establish we.

Hymn 13

Romans 4:2-8

Denfield

1 IF Abraham were justified
     by works which earned reward,
  he had whereof he glory might;
     but not before his God.

2 For what saith scripture? Abr'ham did
     belief in God confess,
  and therefore it imputed was
     to him for righteousness.

3 Now unto him that doeth works
     that wages he might get,

ROMANS

his just reward is not of grace,
   but reckoned as of debt.

4 But to him that works not, but trusts
     on him that reckons just
  the godless man, for righteousness
     imputed is his trust.

5 As David also doth himself
     describe the blessedness
  of him to whom God without works
     imputeth righteousness,

6 Bless'd are they whose iniquities
     forgiven are, saith he,
  yea, even those whose grievous sins
     have covered been by thee.

7 O happy is that man and blessed
     in truth to whom the Lord
  imputeth not his sin, nor doth
     him render just reward.

Hymn 14
Romans 4:13-16
Drumclog

1 TO Abraham, and to his seed,
     the promise made afore,
  that he should heir be of the world,
     was made not through the law;

2 Because that through the righteousness
     of faith it was decreed.
  For if they of the law be heirs,
     then faith is void indeed:

15

3 And, thereby made of none effect,
    the promise is undone.
  Law worketh wrath: where no law is,
    transgression there is none.

4 It therefore is of faith alone,
    that it might be by grace,
  unto the end that all the seed
    the promise might embrace.

Hymn 15
Romans 4:20-25

Wiltshire

1 GOD'S promise Abr'ham did believe,
    and for it waited long;
  he staggered not through unbelief,
    but in his faith was strong;

2 And giving glory unto God,
    he was persuaded too
  that what to him he promised had,
    he able was to do:

3 And therefore it imputed was
    to him for righteousness.
  Now this not only for his sake
    the scripture doth express,

4 That it to him imputed was:
    but we this should receive,
  to whom it shall imputed be
    if on him we believe,

ROMANS

5 E'en he that Jesus, our own Lord,
   from death did raise on high:
   who for offences we had done
   delivered was to die;

6 And through our being justified,
   when he in death had lain,
   was on the third day from the dead
   raised up to life again.

Hymn 16

Romans 5:1-5

S. Bernard

1 NOW therefore having been by faith
   before him justified,
   with God through our Lord Jesus Christ
   in peace we do abide:

2 By whom by faith into this grace
   wherein we stablished be
   we access have: and joy in hope
   God's glory great to see.

3 Not only so, but glory we
   in tribulations too:
   aware from tribulation long
   that patience doth ensue;

4 And patience works experience;
   experience again
   outworks in hope: and, unashamed,
   hope waiteth not in vain;

HYMNS OF THE NEW TESTAMENT

5 Because that by the Holy Ghost,
   which given us hath he,
  the love of God is in our hearts
   shed forth abundantly.

Hymn 17

Romans 5:6, 8-10

Argyle

1 FOR when we yet were without strength,
    and as due time drew nigh,
  Christ came unto us that he might
    for the ungodly die.

2 Toward us God commends his love,
    and hath it magnified,
  in that, whilst we yet sinners were,
    Christ came and for us died.

3 Much more then, being by his blood
    now justified through grace,
  we shall be saved from wrath through him
    who suffered in our place.

4 For if, when we were enemies,
    we then were reconciled,
  brought unto God by his Son's death,
    who were by guilt defiled,

5 Much more then, being reconciled
    by his death in our stead,
  we shall be saved by his own life
    now risen from the dead.

Hymn 18
Romans 5:12, 14-21

S. Anne

1 As sin, and death by sin, the world
    by one man entered in,
  and so death passed upon all men,
    because that all did sin:

2 (From Adam reigned both sin and death,
    all men to overcome.
  Now Adam is the figure true
    of him that was to come.)

3 But not as the offence, so is
    the free gift also seen:
  for if through the offence of one
    there many dead have been,

4 How much more shall the grace of God,
    and gift of grace thereby,
  which is by one man, Jesus Christ,
    to many multiply.

5 And not by one that sinned appears
    the gift that doth abound:
  (because the judgment was by one
    to condemnation found;

6 But after the offences great
    of many multiplied,
  the gift was then made manifest
    that freely justified.)

7 For if by that one man's offence
    death by that one did reign,
  much more they an abundance which
    do of free grace obtain,

8 And of the gift of righteousness,
    shall also reign by one,
  abounding in the life that is
    by Jesus Christ alone.

9 As therefore by the one offence
    the judgment came on all,
  and condemnation strict was passed,
    upon all men to fall;

10 E'en so by the one righteousness
    the gift came which was free
  upon all men, that unto life
    they justified might be.

11 By one man's disobedience
    were many sinners made;
  so many righteous shall become
    because one man obeyed.

12 (The law came in that the offence
    might to increase be found;
  but where sin much abounded, there
    did grace much more abound:)

13 That as sin unto death hath reigned,
    to life eternal grace
  likewise by Jesus Christ our Lord
    might reign through righteousness.

Hymn 19

Romans 6:1-13, 14
Winchester

1 WHAT then? So that grace might abound,
    shall we go on in sin?
  Nay, how shall we, to sin that died,
    live any more therein?

2 All those baptised in Jesus Christ,
    baptised in his death be:
  for buried with him into death
    by baptism are we.

3 As by the Father's glory Christ
    from death was raised again,
  so we should walk in newness that
    doth unto life pertain.

4 If in the likeness of his death
    been planted first have we,
  we of his resurrection too
    shall in the likeness be:

5 For our old man is crucified
    with him, that done away
  might be sin's body, that henceforth
    we should not sin obey.

6 For he that died is freed from sin:
    if dead with Christ we be,
  then we affirm and do believe
    that live with him shall we:

7 Because that Christ, raised up from death,
    can never die again;

death hath no more dominion
  that it o'er him should reign.

8 For he, in that he died, died once,
    and sin he put away:
  but now, in that he lives again,
    he lives to God alway.

9 So likewise reckon ye yourselves
    as dead to sin abhorred,
  and count yourselves alive to God
    through Jesus Christ our Lord.

10 And in your mortal body hence
     let sin no longer reign,
   that in the lusts thereof ye should
     it e'er obey again.

11 Your members neither any more
     as instruments afford
   e'en of unrighteousness to sin:
     but yield yourselves to God.

12 For henceforth sin shall over you
     dominion have no more,
   because that ye are under grace,
     no longer under law.

Hymn 20

Romans 6:15-23 *Forest Green*

1 WHAT shall we say? Shall we in sin
     continue, as we did,
  because we are not under law
    but grace? Nay, God forbid.

ROMANS

2 For know ye not, that unto whom
 yourselves submit do ye
as servants bounden to obey,
 his servants ye shall be:

3 If it should either be of sin,
 which unto death doth reign;
or of obedience that doth
 to righteousness pertain?

4 But God be thanked, that though ye were
 the servants once of sin,
ye are no more in servitude,
 nor bound to serve therein;

5 For from the heart ye have obeyed
 that form of doctrine sound
to you delivered, that your faith
 should in the same be found.

6 And being thus made free from sin,
 the servants ye became
of righteousness, that henceforth ye
 might freely serve the same.

7 As to uncleanness servants then
 your members yielded ye,
and to iniquity again
 unto iniquity;

8 So even now your members yield
 in servitude each day
to righteousness and holiness,
 as servants that obey.

9 For ye, when ye sin's servants were,
   from righteousness were free.
 What fruit then had ye in those things
   whereof now 'shamed ye be?

10 For of those things death is the end:
   but now, as being freed
 from bondage unto sin, to God
   ye servants are indeed;

11 And henceforth unto holiness
   your fruit possess do ye,
 and everlasting life in truth
   the end thereof shall be.

12 For death the wages is of sin;
   but freely sent from God
 the gift is everlasting life
   through Jesus Christ our Lord.

Hymn 21
Romans 8:1-14

Evangel

1 No condemnation falls on them
     that in Christ Jesus be,
 who in the Spirit, not the flesh,
   do walk continually.

2 Because the law of life which from
     the Spirit doth proceed
 hath in Christ Jesus from the law
   of sin and death me freed.

ROMANS

3 For what the law could in no wise
    enable to be done,
  in that it weak was through the flesh,
    God did through his own Son;

4 Whom he did in the likeness send
    of sinful flesh, for sin,
  that sin he in the flesh might judge,
    and it condemn therein:

5 That of the law the righteousness
    in us fulfilled might be,
  who in the flesh walk not, but in
    the Spirit's liberty.

6 They that are of the flesh are all
    to fleshly things inclined;
  but they that of the Spirit be,
    the Spirit's things do mind.

7 For to be minded carnally
    to death doth give increase;
  but to be of the Spirit's mind
    pertains to life and peace.

8 Because the carnal mind 'gainst God
    abides at enmity:
  for 'tis not subject to God's law,
    and neither can it be.

9 To God they that are in the flesh
    no pleasure can afford:
  ye in the Spirit are, if ye
    the Spirit have of God.

HYMNS OF THE NEW TESTAMENT

10 Now if, my brethren, any man
    there found among you is,
which Christ's own Spirit doth not have,
    that man is none of his.

11 The body, if Christ in you be,
    is dead because of sin;
but life, because of righteousness,
    the Spirit is within.

12 But if the Spirit of him that
    did Jesus raise again
up from the dead to life anew
    doth in you all remain,

13 Then he that raised Christ from the dead
    your mortal bodies too
shall quicken by his Spirit that
    doth also dwell in you.

14 So therefore, brethren, debtors made
    not to the flesh are we,
to live therein. If to the flesh
    ye live, then die shall ye:

15 But if ye through the Spirit, whom
    he unto us did give,
the body's deeds do mortify,
    most surely ye shall live.

16 Because as many as in truth
    are led continually
e'en by the Spirit of our God,
    the sons of God they be.

ROMANS

Hymn 22
Romans 8:19-30

S. Bernard

1 THE earnest expectation of
 creation is expressed
in waiting for the sons of God
 to be made manifest.

2 Creation was to vanity
 not willingly abased,
but through him who in hope the same
 hath in subjection placed:

3 For from corruption's bondage shall
 the same delivered be
into the glory that is of
 God's children's liberty.

4 We of creation know that all
 that doth to it pertain
together groaneth until now,
 and travaileth in pain.

5 Not only they, but we ourselves,
 to whom have been made known
the Spirit's first-fruits, even we
 within ourselves do groan;

6 Who do for the adoption wait,
 to wit, that we might see
our body's full redemption wrought
 in perfect liberty.

7 For we by hope are saved: but hope,
    once seen, is hope no more:
  for those things that a man doth see,
    why doth he yet hope for?

8 But if with earnestness we hope
    for that we do not see,
  then for what is invisible
    with patience wait do we.

9 And likewise our infirmities
    the Spirit helps alway:
  because we know not as we should
    for what we ought to pray:

10 But it the Spirit is himself
    that for us makes request
  with intercessions and with groans
    which cannot be expressed.

11 And he the hearts that searcheth doth
    the Spirit's mind know still,
  who intercedeth for the saints
    according to God's will.

12 For good to them that do love God
    together work things all,
  yea, to them whom according to
    his purpose he did call.

13 For whom he did foreknow, the same
    predestinate did he,
  that to the image of his Son
    each one conformed should be;

ROMANS

14 That he 'mong many brethren might
    be first-born named withal.
  For whom he did predestinate,
    them also he did call:

15 Moreover those whom he did call,
    he also justified:
  and those whom he did justify,
    he also glorified.

Hymn 23

Romans 8:31-39

Wondrous Love
(refrain slightly adapted)

1 WHAT shall we say then to these things,
    or what conclude shall we?
  If God himself be on our side,
    who can against us be?

2 He that spared not his Son, but him
    gave up that we might live,
  how shall he also not with him
    us all things freely give?

3 Who shall against us lay one charge,
    or up against us rise?
  who dare accuse God's own elect?
    'Tis God that justifies!

4 Who then is he that doth condemn?
    For it is Christ that died,
  yea, rather, risen from the dead,
    that ever doth abide:

5 Who even is at God's right hand,
    appearing for our sake;
  who also intercession doth
    in heaven for us make.

6 From the abiding love of Christ
    who shall us separate:
  or what shall once between us come
    division to create?

7 Shall tribulation, or distress,
    or persecution sore,
  dearth, nakedness, or jeopardy,
    or yet the sword of war?

8 As it is written, For thy sake
    we killed are all the day:
  as sheep unto the slaughter sent
    account us all do they.

9 But nonetheless in all these things
    that set against us be,
  through him that did us love, far more
    than conquerors are we.

10 Convinced I am that neither death,
    nor life, nor angels great,
  nor principalities, nor powers,
    nor those that do us hate,

11 Nor present things, nor things to come,
    nor height, nor depth withal,
  nor any other creature formed,
    nor anything at all,

ROMANS

12 Shall able be to separate
     us from the love of God,
   which evermore abides in him,
     Christ Jesus, e'en our Lord.

Hymn 24
Romans 9:6-24

S. Magnus

1 FOR they are not all Israel,
     of Isr'el which appear:
   nor, though they are of Abr'ham's seed,
     are they all children dear.

2 For, Called in Isaac is thy seed.
     That is, All they which be
   the children of the flesh are not
     God's children verily.

3 The children of the promise, these
     are counted for the seed.
   For 'tis the promise: I to thee
     will at this time proceed,

4 And Sarah shall a son bring forth.
     And neither this alone,
   but when Rebecca had conceived
     and was of Isaac known;

5 (The unborn children having yet
     no good or evil done,
   according to election that
     God's purpose sure might run,

6 And that it might established be,
   for ever firm to stand,
of him that calleth, not of works;)
   he to her gave command,

7 The elder shall the younger serve.
   As he doth testify,
declaring: Jacob I have loved,
   but Esau hated I.

8 What shall we say then? Is there found
   unrighteousness with God?
Nay, God forbid. For he of old
   by Moses did record:

9 On whom I mercy have, saith he,
   I will have mercy still;
compassion I will have on whom
   compassion have I will.

10 So then 'tis not of him that wills,
   nor man that doth propose,
nor yet of him that runneth, but
   of God that mercy shows.

11 For unto Pharaoh scripture saith,
   'Twas I that gave decree
and raised thee up, e'en for this cause,
   to show my pow'r in thee;

12 And that throughout the earth my name
   the nations all might know.
He therefore mercy hath on whom
   he will his mercy show,

ROMANS

13 And whom he will he hardeneth.
 Thou'lt say to me, Why still
is it that he finds fault? for who
 resisted hath his will?

14 Nay but, O man, and who art thou
 that dost 'gainst God reply?
Shall that thing formed say unto him
 that formed it, Tell me why?

15 Cannot the potter of the clay
 one honoured vessel take,
and of the rest a vessel then
 unto dishonour make?

16 For what if God, who willing was
 abroad his wrath to show,
and to make manifest his might
 that men his pow'r should know;

17 What if, I say, he did with much
 long-suffering endure
the vessels of his wrath, that to
 destruction fitted were;

18 And of his glory that he might
 the riches great make known
upon the vessels that are of
 his mercy called alone,

19 Which he for glory had prepared:
 e'en us, whom he foreknew,
and called, not only of the Jews,
 but of the Gentiles too?

HYMNS OF THE NEW TESTAMENT

Hymn 25
Romans 11:33-36
Lyngham

1 GOD'S wisdom and his knowledge rich
    in depth exceed all praise;
his judgments are unsearchable,
    past finding out his ways.

2 For who is there at any time
    that hath the Lord's mind known?
or who hath been his counsellor
    and wisdom to him shown?

3 Or who hath given first to him
    out of his bounty free,
so that of debt to him again
    it recompensed should be?

4 For of and through him are all things,
    to whom all things pertain:
to whom be glory evermore.
    Amen, yea, and Amen.

Hymn 26
Romans 12:4-8
Duke's Tune

1 FOR as we many members have
    which but one body form,
and as the members all do not
    the selfsame work perform:

2 So, being many, we in Christ
    are as one body seen;

ROMANS

    and with the other every one
    a member made hath been.

3 Then having gifts as differing
    each from the other one,
according to the grace that is
    unto each member shown:

4 If it should be of prophecy,
    then let us prophesy
according to the measure which
    faith doth to each supply;

5 Or ministry, on minist'ring;
    he likewise that doth teach,
on teaching; or he that exhorts,
    upon this wise beseech;

6 He that doth give, then let this with
    simplicity appear;
or he that rules, with diligence;
    or mercy shows, with cheer.

Hymn 27
Romans 16:25-27   *Kedron*

1 NOW unto him that is of power
    to stablish you as one
according to that gospel which
    was unto me made known,

2 And that concerning Jesus Christ
    which preached hath been by me,
after the revelation of
    the hidden mystery,

HYMNS OF THE NEW TESTAMENT

3 Kept secret since the world began,
   but now made manifest,
 and by the scriptures which have been
   in prophecy expressed,

4 According to the due command
   of the eternal God,
 made known for faith's obedience
   to nations all abroad:

5 Now unto God, to whom alone
   all wisdom doth pertain,
 be praise and glory evermore
   through Jesus Christ. Amen.

Hymn 28
I Corinthians 1:4-9

French

1 I TO my God on your behalf
     give thanks each day anew,
 for God's free grace by Jesus Christ
   which given is to you;

2 That ye in everything by him
   enriched are and abound,
 excelling in all utterance,
   and in all knowledge sound;

3 E'en as Christ's testimony was
   confirmed in you each one:
 so that of all the gifts endowed
   ye come behind in none;

I CORINTHIANS

4 While ye of our Lord Jesus Christ
  the coming do await:
who also shall you to the end
  confirm in your estate:

5 That pure and blameless ye may be
  in the forthcoming day
of our Lord Jesus Christ: for God
  is faithful every way,

6 By whom unto the fellowship
  and to the unity
of his Son Jesus Christ our Lord
  together called were ye.

Hymn 29

I Corinthians 1:26-31

Amazing Grace

1 BEHOLD, not many wise men called
    after the flesh there be:
not many mighty, nobles few,
  ye in your calling see.

2 But God hath of the foolish things
    that in the world are found
in truth made choice, that so he might
  those that are wise confound.

3 And God hath chosen from the world
    things weak exceedingly,
that by his choice he might confound
  the things that mighty be.

4 And base things which are of the world,
    and things which are despised,
God chosen hath, and those things which
    are not of men apprized;

5 That so the things which now abide
    to nothing brought might be,
that in his presence there no flesh
    should triumph gloriously.

6 But you he in Christ Jesus called,
    of God our wisdom true,
both righteousness, and holiness,
    yea, and redemption too:

7 That, as the prophet wrote afore,
    according to the word,
What man soever glorieth,
    let glory in the Lord.

Hymn 30

I Corinthians 2:11-14

York

1 THE things that unto man belong
    what man can ascertain,
save by the spirit which to man
    alone doth appertain?

2 So likewise no man knows the things
    belonging unto God,
save that God's Spirit unto him
    the knowledge doth afford.

I CORINTHIANS

3 Now not the spirit of the world
   received of him have we,
  but that same Spirit which with God
   doth dwell in unity:

4 So that with understanding know
   assuredly might we
  the things that freely of our God
   unto us given be.

5 Which things made known we also speak,
   not in the words of speech
  taught by man's wisdom, but those which
   the Holy Ghost doth teach;

6 Comparing things found spiritual
   with spiritual alone.
  But man by nature never doth
   such things receive or own:

7 Things of God's Spirit are to him
   both foolish and unlearn'd,
  nor can he know them, for they by
   the Spirit are discerned.

Hymn 31

I Corinthians 3:16-20

Coleshill

1 NOW, brethren, know ye not yourselves
    that ye God's temple be,
  and that God's Spirit doth in you
   abide continually?

2 If there should any man defile
    the temple of our God,
  then God shall with destruction sore
    that man in wrath reward;

3 Because God's temple holy is,
    which temple pure are ye.
  Let no man therefore of himself
    a vain deceiver be.

4 If any man among you doth
    seem wise in this world's eyes,
  then let him as a fool become,
    so that he may be wise.

5 Because the wisdom of this world
    with God is foolishness.
  For scripture saith, He takes the wise
    in their own craftiness.

6 As in a certain other place
    it written is again,
  The Lord the thoughts knows of the wise,
    that surely they are vain.

Hymn 32

I Corinthians 6:9-11

Gräfenberg

1 MY brethren, be ye not deceived:
    know not in truth do ye
  that the unrighteous never shall
    heirs of God's kingdom be?

I CORINTHIANS

2 The filthy, the idolaters,
    adulterers withal,
effeminate, those with mankind
    into abuse that fall,

3 Thieves, drunkards, railers, covetous,
    extortioners each one,
shall in the kingdom of our God
    inheritance have none.

4 And such, ye know, were some of you:
    but throughly washed are ye,
but ye are also sanctified,
    but justified ye be;

5 For this in the Lord Jesus' name
    is unto you assured,
and by the Spirit that through him
    is sent forth of our God.

HYMN 33

I Corinthians 10:1-12

Hermon

1 MOREOVER, brethren, I would not
    that ye deceived should be:
our fathers all dwelt 'neath the cloud,
    and all passed through the sea;

2 And in the cloud and sea baptised
    to Moses were they all;
and of the same meat spiritual
    each one did eat withal;

HYMNS OF THE NEW TESTAMENT

3 And of the same drink spiritual
      they drank: for drink did they
of that same Rock (which Rock was Christ)
      which followed in their way.

4 But unto many of them God
      made his displeasure known:
for they amidst the wilderness
      by him were overthrown.

5 Now these things our examples were,
      to the intent that we
should lust not after evil things,
      as they did constantly.

6 Nor be idolaters like them;
      as doth the scripture say,
The people sat to eat and drink,
      and rose up for to play.

7 And neither let us fornicate,
      as some of them did then,
and fell in but one day some three
      and twenty thousand men.

8 And neither let us now tempt Christ,
      as some of them did err
when him they tempted, so that they
      destroyed of serpents were.

9 Nor murmur ye, as some their tongues
      in murmuring employed,
upon whom the destroyer came,
      so that they were destroyed.

I CORINTHIANS

10 Now for ensamples unto us
  these things did them befall,
that we, on whom the world's ends come,
  should be admonished all.

Hymn 34
I Corinthians 10:16-17

Repton

1 THE cup of blessing, brethren, which
    in unity we bless,
  doth it not the communion
    of Christ's own blood express?

2 So with the bread together which
    we break in unity,
  do we not the communion
    of Christ's own body see?

3 For we, though many, are one bread,
    and as one body seen:
  because as one we of that bread
    have all partakers been.

Hymn 35
I Corinthians 11:1-15

Tallis

1 MY brethren, as I follow Christ,
    be followers of me.
  Now you I praise that in all things
    remember me do ye;

43

2 For ye the ordinances keep
    which I to you did show.
  But I moreover, brethren, this
    would also have you know:

3 That over every man of you
    Christ is the head assured,
  and of the woman man is head,
    the head of Christ is God.

4 Each man in prayer or prophecy,
    that any matter saith,
  whilst having cover on his head,
    his head dishonoureth.

5 But every woman who to pray
    or prophesy is led,
  whilst still her head uncovered is,
    dishonoureth her head:

6 For that as if she shaven were
    is counted all as one.
  For if she will uncovered be,
    let her be also shorn.

7 But if it be a shameful thing
    a woman for to see
  that either shorn or shaven is,
    then let her covered be.

8 For covered never should a man
    allow his head to be,
  because of God the image and
    the glory true is he.

I CORINTHIANS

9 The woman is man's glory since
      all things at first began.
   For of the woman man is not,
      but woman of the man.

10 Nor yet created was the man
      the woman's for to be,
   because the woman so was formed
      that be the man's might she.

11 And for this cause the woman ought
      authority to show
   upon her head: for angels high
      observe all things below.

12 Without the woman nonetheless
      the man is incomplete;
   nor is the woman, in the Lord,
      without the man complete.

13 For as unto the woman man
      did being first afford;
   man by the woman being hath:
      but all things are of God.

14 How can it be a comely thing,
      judge in yourselves do ye,
   that unto God a woman pray
      if she uncovered be?

15 For doth not nature in itself
      this doctrine, too, proclaim,
   that, if a man should have long hair,
      it is to him a shame?

HYMNS OF THE NEW TESTAMENT

16 But if a woman have long hair,
    her glory is in this;
behold, her hair is given her:
    a covering it is.

17 Thus nature by the hair itself
    doth teach what hath been said,
The man must not, the woman must,
    wear cover on the head.

HYMN 36
I Corinthians 11:23-26
S. Columba

1 THAT which I of the Lord received
    I also to you said,
That the Lord Jesus in the night
    he was betrayed took bread:

2 And giving thanks, he did it break.
    Take, eat: for this, said he,
my broken body is: this do
    in memory of me.

3 He in like manner took the cup
    when he had supped, and said,
This cup is the new testament
    in my blood for you shed:

4 This do ye, he declared, as oft
    as drink of it ye shall,
that ye together me thereby
    may to remembrance call.

5 Because as oft as eat this bread
and drink this cup do ye,
the Lord's death ye make manifest,
till come again shall he.

Hymn 37
I Corinthians 12:4-11

Jackson

1 THERE are diversities of gifts:
the Spirit is the same.
Administrations differ, but
one Lord they all proclaim.

2 And there are operations which
for diverse forms do call,
but yet it is the selfsame God
which worketh all in all.

3 But that which of the Spirit is
made manifest and plain,
is given unto every man
that all may profit gain.

4 The word of wisdom unto one
the Spirit doth afford;
another by that Spirit hath
the knowledge of the word;

5 And that same Spirit doth to one
the gift of faith present;
and to another healing gifts,
by that same Spirit sent;

6 The gift of working miracles
he to another sends;

HYMNS OF THE NEW TESTAMENT

and, lo, the gift of prophecy
    another apprehends;
7 Another spirits doth discern;
    another doth excel
in kinds of tongues; another doth
    interpretation tell:

8 But all these worketh but that one
    and selfsame Spirit still,
who sev'rally to every man
    divideth as he will.

HYMN 38
I Corinthians 12:12-28

Moravia

1 AS in the body's unity
      there many members be,
and in that body's members' sum
    we but one body see,

2 So also doth the Christ appear.
    For we, whom he did call,
by that one Spirit are baptised
    into one body all:

3 Though Jew or Gentile we be called,
    or whether bond or free;
into one Spirit, every one,
    been made to drink have we.

4 For of itself no member can
    the body form alone,
but many members differing
    the body form in one.

I CORINTHIANS

5 If saith the foot, Since I the hand
     am not in verity,
   I'm of the body not; can it
     not of the body be?

6 And should the ear say, Since I am
     not made to be the eye,
   I'm of the body not; doth it
     not in the body lie?

7 If all the body were an eye,
     what sounds would be received?
   If all were hearing, by what means
     would smelling be achieved?

8 But now God in the body hath
     the members set each one,
   in that, according to his will,
     what pleased him he hath done.

9 If they were all one member, where
     were its diversity?
   But now, though but one body, they
     full many members be.

10 The eye can say not, Thou'rt, O hand,
     not needed by the eye:
   nor can the head say to the feet,
     No need of you have I.

11 Nay, how much more those members that
     are in the body set,
   which seem to be the feeblest ones,
     are necessary yet.

49

HYMNS OF THE NEW TESTAMENT

12 And of the body those we think
    of honour less in need,
on such bestow we honour more
    abundantly indeed;

13 And our uncomely parts have more
    abundant comeliness.
Because of honour no such need
    our comely parts possess.

14 But to his will God hath so made
    the body to conform,
that he hath given honour more
    to that which lacked in form:

15 That in the body's unity
    we might all schism shun;
but that the members should have care
    each for the other one.

16 And if one member suffer, then
    all members suff'ring bear;
or one be honoured, all with it
    the same rejoicing share.

17 Now ye the body are of Christ,
    and members all are ye
which in particular appear
    within its unity.

18 And God hath in the church set some:
    the first, apostles true;
and second, prophets; teachers, third;
    and then, in order due,

I CORINTHIANS

19 Both miracles, and healings' gifts,
    with helps that strength supply,
next governments, and kinds of tongues,
    the whole to edify.

Hymn 39

I Corinthians 13:1-8

S. Agnes

1 THOUGH I with men's and angels' tongues
    should speak, and have not love,
then I as sounding brass or as
    a tinkling cymbal prove.

2 And though I from above the gift
    of prophecy receive,
and understand all mysteries,
    and knowledge all perceive;

3 And though I have all faith, so that
    I mountains could remove;
for all these things I nothing am,
    if I possess not love.

4 Though all my goods to feed the poor
    I without love bestow,
and give my body to be burned,
    no profit doth it show.

5 Love in its nature suffers long,
    and is exceeding kind;
love envies not, vaunts not itself,
    is not puffed up in mind;

6 Unseemly it doth not behave;
   her own she doth not seek;
 she is not easily provoked,
   nor hastily doth speak;

7 No evil thinketh, neither joys
   iniquity to see;
 but all her joy is in the truth,
   for all things beareth she,

8 All things believeth, all things hopes;
   all things she doth endure.
 Love never faileth, love indeed
   abideth evermore.

Hymn 40
I Corinthians 14:26-31

Bristol

1 WHEN, brethren, ye together meet,
     how is it you among?
 Each one a psalm or doctrine hath,
     another hath a tongue;

2 Or each a revelation hath
     of which to testify;
 another this interpreteth:
     let all things edify.

3 If speech be in an unknown tongue,
     by two let this be done,
 or three at most, and that by course:
     interpret let but one.

4 If none interpret, in the church
     then let him silent be;

I CORINTHIANS

but to himself and unto God
   speak certainly may he.

5 And let the prophets, two or three,
   a faithful witness bear;
and let the others that give ear
   their judgment just declare.

6 If to another sitting by,
   when prophecy doth cease,
there anything should be revealed,
   the first let hold his peace.

7 Because ye all may prophesy,
   but one by one in turn,
so that all may be comforted,
   and every one may learn.

Hymn 41
I Corinthians 15:51-57

Nearer Home (short metre)

1 BEHOLD, I unto you
   do show a mystery:
Not all of us shall fall asleep,
   but changed we all shall be;

2 In but a moment swift,
   that instantly is past,
as in the twinkling of an eye,
   when sounds the trumpet blast.

3 For sound the trumpet shall,
   and raised the dead shall be

with bodies incorruptible,
and changed become shall we.

4 For this corruptible
    must incorruption bear,
and clothed with immortality
    this mortal must appear.

5 When incorruptible
    shall this corruption be,
and when this mortal shall put on
    her immortality:

6 Then shall be brought to pass
    the word that scripture saith,
Rejoice do ye, for swallowed up
    in victory is death.

7 O death, where is thy sting?
    O grave, thy victory?
The sting of death is sin, the strength
    of sin the law's decree.

8 But now and evermore
    to God thanksgiving be,
who gives through our Lord Jesus Christ
    to us the victory.

Hymn 42

II Corinthians 2:14-17 *University*

1 NOW thanks be unto God in Christ,
        who manifests by grace
the savour of his knowledge pure
    by us in every place.

II CORINTHIANS

2 For unto God are we of Christ
    a savour sweet and true,
 not only in them that are saved,
    but them that perish too:

3 Unto the one the savour made
    of death to death are we;
 but to the other we of life
    to life the savour be.

4 Who of himself can for such things
    sufficiency afford?
 For we are not as many which
    corrupt the word of God:

5 Nay, but as of sincerity,
    but as of God alone,
 as alway in the sight of God,
    our speech in Christ is known.

Hymn 43
II Corinthians 3:3-6

S. Mirren

1 YE the epistle are of Christ
    which ministered have we;
 for written with the Spirit of
    the living God ye be:

2 Not as in tables made of stone,
    but fleshy, of the heart;
 and we such trust to Godward have
    through Christ this to impart.

3 Not that sufficient of ourselves
    to think something are we

as of ourselves, because of God
   is our sufficiency;
4 Who also able ministers
   hath called us forth to be,
that thereby the new testament
   administer might we;

5 Not of the letter dead, but of
   the Spirit which doth live:
because the letter killeth, but
   the Spirit life doth give.

Hymn 44

II Corinthians 3:7-18 — *S. James*

1 BUT if of death the ministry
      in stones engraved of old
   was glorious, that Moses' face
      they could no more behold,

2 In that his face with glory shone,
      which glory should decline:
   how shall the Spirit's ministry
      not more in glory shine?

3 If glory did the ministry
      of condemnation light,
   much more doth that of righteousness
      exceed in glory bright.

4 Of that which was made glorious
      none could the glory tell,
   in this respect, because of that
      which should the more excel:

II CORINTHIANS

5 For if that which is done away
    such glory did obtain,
  how much more glory hath that which
    shall evermore remain!

6 As seeing then that from these things
    we such a hope possess,
  we therefore in the speech we use
    great plainness do express:

7 Not as when Moses veiled his face,
    that Isr'el steadfastly
  could look not to the end of that
    which should abolished be.

8 But blind their minds were: for that veil
    remains until this day
  in reading the old testament
    untaken still away;

9 Which veil is done away in Christ.
    But to this day 'tis plain,
  when Moses' word is read, the veil
    doth on their heart remain.

10 When nonetheless it shall to turn
     unto the Lord be moved,
   the veil shall taken be away
     and from the heart removed.

11 Now then, the Lord that Spirit is,
     and whereso found shall be
   the Spirit that is of the Lord,
     then there is liberty.

HYMNS OF THE NEW TESTAMENT

12 But yet we all with open face
  beholding, not in vain,
as in a glass the glory that
  doth to the Lord pertain,

13 Are into that same image changed,
  without a veil obscured,
from glory unto glory by
  the Spirit of the Lord.

Hymn 45
II Corinthians 4:1-6

Kilsyth

1 NOW since we have this ministry
  entrusted to our care,
e'en as we mercy have received,
  we faint not nor despair;

2 But have renounced the hidden things
  of guile; nor walked have we
in craftiness, nor handled once
  God's word deceitfully;

3 But by the truth made manifest
  ourselves we do commend
as in God's sight, that we no man
  in conscience should offend.

4 But if the gospel which we preach
  from any hidden be,
it is unto them that are lost
  hid in obscurity:

II CORINTHIANS

5 In whom the god that's of this world,
   which did the same deceive,
hath blinded and obscured the minds
   of them which disbelieve,

6 Lest that the glorious gospel light,
   which forth from Christ doth shine,
who is of God the image true,
   should unto them incline.

7 For we preach not ourselves, but preach
   Christ Jesus as the Lord,
and do our service unto you
   for Jesus' sake afford.

8 For God, from out of darkness deep
   who did command the light
that it should shine, within our hearts
   hath shined exceeding bright;

9 That of God's glory's knowledge true
   the light give forth might he,
which in the face of Jesus Christ
   doth shine abundantly.

Hymn 46

II Corinthians 4:16-18

Arnold

1 FOR this cause faint we not, although
      our outward man decay,
   because the inward man in strength
      renewed is day by day.

2 Our light affliction, which but for
  a moment doth endure,
works for us an exceeding weight
  of glory evermore;

3 Whilst in our earthly pilgrimage
  we look not at things seen,
but earnestly in spirit view
  the things that are unseen:

4 Things which are seen are temporal,
  and have no longer stay;
but things unseen eternal are,
  and never pass away.

Hymn 47

II Corinthians 5:10-11

Lynton

1 BEFORE the judgment-seat of Christ
  we soon must all appear,
that every one in that great day
  the sentence due might hear,

2 According to that he hath done
  when in the body found;
for whether it were good or bad,
  the judgment just shall sound.

3 The terror knowing of the Lord,
  we therefore men persuade:
for manifest are we to God
  and to your conscience made.

II CORINTHIANS

Hymn 48
II Corinthians 5:14-21
None but Christ can Satisfy + refrain

1 THE love of Christ constraineth us,
      because thus judge do we:
   that if for all one died, then all
      were reckoned dead to be.

2 He died for all, that they which live
      alive should not remain
   unto themselves, but unto him
      which died and rose again.

3 Wherefore after the flesh know we
      no man as heretofore:
   though we have so known Christ, henceforth
      now know we him no more.

4 If any man be found in Christ,
      a creature new is he:
   old things are passed away; behold,
      all things made new shall be.

5 Moreover all things are of God,
      who hath his favour shown,
   and reconciled us to himself,
      by Jesus Christ alone:

6 And also freely given hath
      to us the ministry
   of reconciliation which
      made known to you have we;

7 To wit, that God in Christ the world
    then reconciling was
unto himself, imputing not
    to them their trespasses;

8 And hath moreover unto us
    committed that same word
of reconciliation which
    by us is preached abroad.

9 Now we are Christ's ambassadors,
    that God beseech you may
by us: to God be reconciled,
    we in Christ's stead you pray.

10 For he hath made him sin for us,
    although no sin knew he;
that so the righteousness of God
    be made in him might we.

Hymn 49

II Corinthians 6:1-2

Brother James' Air

1 WE then, as fellow-labourers,
    would also you constrain,
that ye the grace that is of God
    should not receive in vain.

2 For in a time accepted I
    have heard thee cry, saith he,
and in salvation's day gave I
    my succour unto thee.

II CORINTHIANS

3 Behold, that the accepted time
   is at this present hour;
   behold, salvation is this day
   put forth in gospel power.

Hymn 50

II Corinthians 6:4-10

Denfield

1 WE as the ministers of God
      approved in all things be:
   in patience much, afflictions sore,
      in all necessity,

2 In great distresses, many stripes,
      and in imprisonments,
   in tumults, labours, watchings oft,
      in fasts and abstinence;

3 By pureness, and by knowledge sound,
      by much long-suff'ring too,
   by kindness, by the Holy Ghost,
      by love unfeigned and true,

4 As by the very word of truth,
      as by God's pow'r to stand,
   by armour forged through righteousness
      supplied on either hand,

5 By honour and dishonour, yea,
      by ill report and good:
   as called deceivers, and yet true,
      though oft misunderstood;

6 As those unknown, and yet well known;
    as dying while we live;
  as chastened, but not killed; as sad,
    yet having joy to give;

7 As poor, yet making many rich;
    as having nothing sure,
  yet in possession of all things,
    both now and evermore.

Hymn 51
II Corinthians 6:17 - 7:1

Kilmarnock

1 O COME ye out, be separate,
    ye that have 'mong them been:
  thus saith the Lord, and touch ye not
    the thing that is unclean;

2 And I will you receive, and will
    a Father to you be,
  the Lord Almighty saith, and sons
    and daughters be shall ye.

3 Beloved, with these promises,
    let us ourselves make clean
  from all the filthiness that is
    in flesh and spirit seen;

4 That we may holiness perfect
    according to his word,
  united with sobriety
    as in the fear of God.

Hymn 52

II Corinthians 10:3-5

Glasgow

1. ALTHOUGH we in the flesh do walk,
    not after it fight we:
  for neither carnal, nor of man,
    our warfare's weapons be;

2. But mighty through our God is that
    with which to war we go,
  unto the pulling down of all
    the strongholds of the foe;

3. Imaginations casting down,
    and every haughty thing
  that 'gainst God's knowledge doth itself
    into contention bring;

4. And bringing every lofty thought
    into captivity,
  that all our reasoning to Christ
    obedient should be.

Hymn 53

II Corinthians 11:2-4, 13-15

Wigtown

1. UNTO one husband you I have
    espoused against that day:
  so that you as a virgin chaste
    to Christ present I may.

2. But fear I, lest by any means,
    as did the serpent Eve

HYMNS OF THE NEW TESTAMENT

    beguile through craft and subtlety,
      so you he might deceive;

3 That from simplicity in Christ
    your minds corrupt might he.
  For if a Jesus false one preach,
    whom never preached have we,

4 Or if a spirit false ye own,
    which ye have not received,
or yet another gospel hear,
    which ye have not believed:

5 Beware! Such false apostles be,
    deceitful workers all,
transformed into their likeness whom
    Christ did apostles call.

6 No marvel this; for Satan too
    makes his appearance bright,
transformed into the likeness of
    an angel filled with light.

7 'Tis therefore no great thing if those
    whom ministers calls he,
as ministers of righteousness
    transformed should also be.

HYMN 54

Galatians 1:1-5

Irish

1 PAUL, an apostle, (not of men,
    and neither by man's call,
but sent by Jesus Christ, and God
    the Father over all,

GALATIANS

2 Who raised him from among the dead;)
 and brethren all with me,
unto the churches of the parts
 that in Galatia be:

3 From God the Father may all grace
 and peace be unto you,
yea, and from our Lord Jesus Christ,
 raised up from death anew:

4 Who did himself give for our sins,
 thereby to set us free,
that from this present evil world
 we might delivered be,

5 After the will that unto God
 our Father doth pertain:
to whom all glory be ascribed
 for evermore. Amen.

Hymn 55
Galatians 1:6-12

Culross

1 FROM him that called you to Christ's grace,
 a marvel 'tis to me,
that ye so soon removed unto
 another gospel be:

2 Which not another gospel is;
 but some would you subvert,
which troublers be, and with deceit
 Christ's gospel would pervert.

3 Though preach we, or an angel bright,
    whom ye from heaven see,
 another gospel than we preached,
    let him accursed be.

4 If one another gospel preach
    than that received at first,
 as we have said, I say again,
    let that man be accurs'd.

5 For now persuade I men, or God?
    or men do I appease?
 For I should not Christ's servant be
    if men I yet should please.

6 But, brethren, you I certify,
    and speak with verity,
 Not after man that gospel came
    which preached hath been by me.

7 For I received it not from man,
    nor was by man it shown,
 but it revealed was unto me
    through Jesus Christ alone.

Hymn 56
Galatians 2:16, 18-21 *Martyrdom*

1 WE know that none is justified
      by deeds wrought through the law;
 but by the faith of Jesus Christ,
    which unto faith is sure;

2 Believed have we in Jesus Christ,
    that by Christ's faith might we

GALATIANS

    be justified, and not by works,
        by which none just shall be.

3 For if I build again the things
      which once destroy did I,
  as one that doth transgress anew
      I make myself thereby.

4 For even through the law itself
      I dead am to the law,
  that I from henceforth unto God
      might live for evermore.

5 For I am crucified with Christ,
      but nonetheless I live;
  yet 'tis no longer I, but Christ,
      that life to me doth give:

6 And in the flesh the life I live
      live by the faith do I
  of God's own Son, in love for me
      who gave himself to die.

7 For I do not frustrate the grace
      which doth to God pertain:
  for if by law comes righteousness,
      then Christ is dead in vain.

HYMN 57

Galatians 3:6-9

Colchester

1 FOR Abraham believed in God,
      and did his faith confess,
  and it in truth accounted was
      to him for righteousness.

2 Whence know ye therefore that all they
 which are of faith indeed
are children unto Abraham,
 and counted for the seed.

3 For, seeing that God would through faith
 the heathen justify,
the scripture did the gospel first
 to Abr'ham testify,

4 In thee shall nations all be bless'd.
 So from the same we see,
that bless'd with faithful Abraham
 are they of faith which be.

Hymn 58

Galatians 3:10-13

Grafton

1 As many as are of the law
 of works and legal deeds
must also come beneath the curse,
 for thus the scripture reads,

2 Whoso continues not to do
 all things that written be
within the pages of the law,
 accurs'd is verily.

3 For that none shall be justified
 in God's sight by the law,
'tis evident: because, By faith
 life to the just is sure.

4 And yet the law is not of faith:
 but rather it doth say,

GALATIANS

That man shall also live in them
  that doth the same obey.

5 Christ hath redeemed us from the curse,
  for made a curse was he:
as written 'tis, Curs'd is each one
  that hangeth on a tree.

Hymn 59
Galatians 3:16-19

S. David

1 TO Abraham and to his seed
    the promises were made.
  Now not of Seeds, but of the Seed,
    e'en Christ, these things were said.

2 The covenant, of God in Christ
    which was confirmed before,
  was thirty and four hundred years
    precedent to the law.

3 And hence the law cannot the oath
    once disannul or break,
  that it the promise pledged of old
    of none effect should make.

4 If law brings in the heritage,
    of promise 'tis no more:
  but God it gave to Abraham
    by promise, not the law.

5 Then wherefore serves the law at all?
    of us is asked by some.
  To curb transgressions added 'twas,
    until the seed should come.

HYMNS OF THE NEW TESTAMENT

HYMN 60
Galatians 3:21-23

Barrow

1 AGAINST the promises of God
      which to the fathers came,
is then the law at variance?
      Nay; God forbid the same.

2 For if a law which could give life
      had given been before,
then verily should righteousness
      have been by that same law.

3 But scripture all 'neath sin concludes,
      that those that do believe
e'en by the faith of Jesus Christ
      the promise might receive.

4 But ere faith came, beneath the law
      kept every one were we,
shut up to faith which afterwards
      to us revealed should be.

HYMN 61
Galatians 4:1-7

Drumclog

1 THE heir, so long as him a child
      the father still doth call,
doth from a servant differ not,
      though he be lord of all;

2 But strictly under tutors kept
      and governors is he,

GALATIANS

    until the time appointed that
        the father doth decree.

3 So, when we were in childhood, we
        in bondage were to fear,
    kept under those same elements
        that in the world appear.

4 But when of time the fulness came
        that promised was afore,
    God sent his Son, of woman made,
        made also under law:

5 That those that 'neath the law were found
        redeem at last might he,
    so that the place of chosen sons
        receive of him might we.

6 And since ye sons are, God hath sent
        the Spirit of his Son,
    which crieth, Abba, Father, forth
        into your hearts each one.

7 Wherefore a servant thou art not:
        a son thou art indeed;
    and if a son, an heir of God,
        through Christ, the promised seed.

Hymn 62
Galatians 4:22-31
Moravia

1 OF Abr'ham it is written that
        two sons beget did he:
    one by a bondmaid, and the next
        born of a woman free.

HYMNS OF THE NEW TESTAMENT

2 After the flesh the bondmaid was,
    and so her child was born.
  The woman free by promise bare,
    her child by oath was sworn.

3 Which things an allegory are:
    two covenants are here;
  one from mount Sinai, gendering
    to bondage and to fear:

4 For Hagar for mount Sinai stands,
    Arabia is she,
  Jerus'lem which now is, in which
    all her bondchildren be.

5 But that Jerusalem above
    is free, and freely bears;
  yea, truly she the mother is
    of all the free-born heirs.

6 It written is of her, Rejoice,
    thou barren, childless one;
  do thou break forth and cry aloud:
    for thou shalt have a son!

7 For she that once was desolate
    hath many children more
  than she which did an husband have
    and fruitful was before.

8 As Isaac, we of promise are:
    but as he was reviled,
  so all the Spirit-born are thus
    vexed by the fleshly child.

GALATIANS

9 What, nonetheless, doth scripture say?
   The bondmaid and her son
cast out from the inheritance:
   'tis for the free-born one!

10 So, brethren all, born from above,
    that of the promise be,
not of the bondmaid are we sons,
    but children of the free.

Hymn 63

Galatians 5:16-18, 22-25

Sawley

1 NOW say I, brethren, Let your walk
     e'er in the Spirit be,
and in the flesh the lust that dwells
   no more fulfil shall ye.

2 Because against the Spirit lusts
     the flesh in enmity,
and 'gainst the flesh the Spirit is,
   for they are contrary:

3 So that ye cannot do the things
     ye would have done before.
But if the Spirit doth you lead,
   ye are not under law.

4 Now from the Spirit is the fruit
     of love and joy and peace,
which with long-suff'ring, gentleness,
   and goodness, doth increase;

5 And with all these doth faith abound,
     and meekness furthermore,
   besides the fruit of temperance:
     'gainst such there is no law.

6 And they that truly are Christ's own
     the flesh have crucified,
   with the affections and the lusts
     that do therein abide.

7 If in the Spirit it be true
     that live indeed do we,
   then in the Spirit let our walk
     from henceforth also be.

Hymn 64

Galatians 6:14-16

Lydia

1 BUT God forbid that I should boast,
     save that I might thereby
   the cross of our Lord Jesus Christ
     exalt and magnify;

2 By whom the world is crucified
     and counted dead to me,
   and also dead unto the world
     I reckoned am to be.

3 For in Christ Jesus nothing doth
     avail that man can do,
   nor circumcision, nor its lack,
     but a creation new.

4 As many as by this rule walk
    shall in the way excel:
on them shall peace and mercy be,
    and on God's Israel.

Hymn 65

Ephesians 1:3-6

Newington

1 OF our Lord Jesus Christ the God
    and Father blessed be,
for in the places heavenly
    us blessed in Christ hath he,

2 Yea, with all blessings spiritual:
    as he his choice hath made
of us in him before that he
    the world's foundation laid;

3 That holy and unblamed in love
    we should before him be:
having predestinated us
    that be his sons might we,

4 Adopting us by Jesus Christ,
    his purpose to fulfil,
after the pleasure good that is
    according to his will;

5 That of the glory of his grace
    the praise fulfilled might be,
wherein in the beloved one
    accepted us hath he.

HYMN 66
Ephesians 1:7-14

Forest Green

1 REDEMPTION have we through his blood,
    our sins' forgiveness free,
  according to the riches which
    in grace made known hath he:

2 Whence he to us abounded hath
    in wisdom prudently,
  as having of his will to us
    made known the mystery,

3 According to his pleasure good
    which in himself he willed:
  that, when the dispensation of
    the times should be fulfilled,

4 He might together gather up
    all things in Christ alone,
  things both in heaven and on earth,
    in him, I say, in one.

5 For in him an inheritance
    obtained withal have we,
  whom after his own purpose sure
    predestinate did he,

6 According to his mighty work
    that doth all things fulfil,
  conforming to the counsel wise
    of his own perfect will:

7 That we should to his glory's praise
    henceforth for ever be,

for first to put in Christ our trust
  and confidence were we.

8 In whom ye also trusted, when
    of truth ye heard the word;
  when first by us the gospel ye
    of your salvation heard:

9 In whom ye also, after that
    believe on him did ye,
  were with that holy Spirit sealed,
    which promised long hath he;

10 Which is of our inheritance
    the earnest rich and free,
  until, unto his glory's praise,
    redeemed the purchase be.

HYMN 67
Ephesians 1:15-23   *Evangel*

1 WHEREFORE I also, after that
    I of your faith did hear
  in the Lord Jesus, and the love
    which to all saints ye bear,

2 Cease not for you my thanks to give
    in all of your affairs,
  whilst making mention oftentimes
    of you in all my prayers.

3 The God of our Lord Jesus Christ,
    which is the Father true
  of glory, now the spirit give
    of wisdom unto you,

4 And revelation, that of him
     the knowledge have may ye,
   and that your understanding's eyes
     may so enlightened be,

5 That ye may know his calling's hope,
     and what the riches be
   which of the glory in the saints
     by heritage hath he,

6 And how, to usward who believe,
     his pow'r exceedeth all,
   according to the working of
     his mighty pow'r withal,

7 Which he in Christ did work, when him
     he raised by his command,
   and him in places heavenly
     set at his own right hand,

8 Above all principality,
     pow'r, might, and high degree,
   and every name named in this world,
     and that world yet to be:

9 And hath put all things 'neath his feet
     that reign o'er all might he,
   and over all things to the church
     gave him the head to be;

10 Which he that is on high above
     doth his own body call,
   the fulness of him that himself
     doth fill all things in all.

Hymn 68
Ephesians 2:1-9   *Amazing Grace*

1 THOUGH dead in trespasses and sins,
    yet quickened you hath he;
  though once according to the course
    of this world walk did ye,

2 According to his pow'r that prince
    o'er all the air is made,
  the spirit working in the sons
    of those that disobeyed:

3 Among whom also had we all
    our conversation vain,
  in times gone past, spent in the lusts
    that to the flesh pertain,

4 Fulfilling the desires that do
    in flesh and mind occur;
  by nature children born of wrath,
    as others also were.

5 But God, who in his mercy kind
    exceeding rich doth prove,
  for his abundant love wherewith
    he greatly did us love,

6 Yea, even when we dead in sins
    were seen by him to be,
  hath quickened us as one with Christ,
    (for saved by grace are ye;)

7 And hath together raised us up,
    and made us sit on high,

together in Christ Jesus found
   in places heavenly:
8 That in the ages yet to come
      his grace show forth might he,
   in kindness through Christ Jesus that
      is rich exceedingly.

9 For ye by grace are saved through faith,
      and that not of yourselves:
   God's gift it is, and not of works,
      lest any boast themselves.

Hymn 69
Ephesians 2:13, 16-22

S. Matthew

1 BUT in Christ Jesus ye who once
      far off in sin did lie,
   are even by the blood of Christ
      unto him now made nigh.

2 For reconciling us to God,
      our peace become is he,
   who in one body by the cross
      hath slain the enmity.

3 And therefore came he preaching peace,
      and did to you appear
   which were far off, yea, and he came
      unto them that were near.

4 For thus together access we
      do have through him alone,
   unto the Father, e'en as by
      the Spirit ever one.

EPHESIANS

5 No longer therefore foreigners
    and strangers now are ye,
  but fellow-citizens with saints
    that of God's household be;

6 And are on the foundation built
    made by the prophets known
  and the apostles, Jesus Christ
    himself chief corner-stone;

7 In whom the building groweth up,
    together fitly framed,
  an holy temple e'en in him
    that Lord of all is named:

8 In whom ye also builded are,
    so that together ye
  might through the Spirit unto God
    an habitation be.

Hymn 70

Ephesians 3:9, 11-21

Salzburg

1 THE fellowship which doth pertain
    unto the mystery,
  which hidden was in God, I, Paul,
    make manifest to be:

2 According to the purpose that
    eternal is and sure,
  which in Christ Jesus, e'en our Lord,
    was purposed heretofore:

HYMNS OF THE NEW TESTAMENT

3 In whom we boldness do possess
    and access that is free,
for entrance by the faith of him
    with confidence have we.

4 Whence at my tribulations all,
    which I for you endure,
which is your glory, I desire
    that ye should faint no more.

5 And for this cause I bow my knees,
    yea, intercede do I,
unto the Father of our Lord,
    e'en Jesus Christ, on high,

6 Who the whole family by name
    in heav'n and earth doth call,
that by his glory's riches he
    would grant unto you all,

7 That by his Spirit with all might
    be wholly filled may ye,
so that ye in the inner man
    might thereby strengthened be;

8 That Christ within your hearts by faith
    may dwell as from above;
that, being rooted by his grace,
    and grounded firm in love,

9 Ye might together able be
    to comprehend aright
with all the saints what is the breadth,
    and length, and depth, and height;

EPHESIANS

10 And so to know the love of Christ,
    which knowledge doth exceed,
that even with God's fulness all
    ye might be filled indeed.

11 Now unto him that is of power
    to do abundantly
above all speech or thought, by that
    which work in us doth he,

12 Yea, by Christ Jesus unto him
    let glory appertain
throughout all ages, in the church,
    world without end. Amen.

Hymn 71
Ephesians 4:1-6

Abbey

1 I PAUL, the pris'ner of the Lord,
    beseech you all that ye
of that vocation worthy walk
    whereunto called ye be,

2 Filled with all lowliness of mind,
    and meekness from above,
abounding with long-suffering,
    forbearing all in love;

3 Endeavouring each one of you
    with steadfast constancy
to keep as in the bond of peace
    the Spirit's unity.

4 For there is but one body seen,
    as we one Spirit own,
just as ye of your calling are
    called in one hope alone;

5 One Lord, one faith, one baptism,
    one God and Father true,
who is above all, and through all,
    and in each one of you.

Hymn 72

Ephesians 4:10-16

None but Christ can Satisfy + refrain

1 THE same that did descend is he
        that did ascend above,
  far o'er all heavens, so that he
        might fill all things in love.

2 Some, first, he as apostles gave;
        and some, his prophets true;
  evangelists; and pastors, some,
        and teachers gave he too;

3 That for the saints' perfecting he
        might thereby gifts ordain,
  for all the work that doth unto
        the ministry pertain;

4 That to the edifying of
        Christ's body this might be:
  till all shall come with one accord
        into faith's unity:

EPHESIANS

5 Till to the knowledge we attain,
    and do the stature span,
 of him who is the Son of God,
    unto a perfect man,

6 As unto that full measure brought
    which in himself he willed,
 to reach the stature true of Christ,
    with all his fulness filled.

7 That children we no more should be,
    as those tossed to and fro,
 and carried off with every wind
    of doctrine that doth blow;

8 As taken by the sleight of men
    of cunning craft that be,
 whilst to deceive they lie in wait
    to catch us privily;

9 But speaking forth the truth in love,
    that into him we may
 grow up in all things, even Christ,
    which is the head, I say:

10 From whom the body, as a whole,
    together fitly joined
 by that which every joint supplies,
    compacted and conjoined,

11 According to the working which,
    effectual in its role,
 within the measure of each part
    contributes to the whole,

HYMNS OF THE NEW TESTAMENT

12 Thus maketh increase bodily,
    in him who is above,
unto the edifying growth
    wrought of itself in love.

Hymn 73

Ephesians 4:17-24 *Beatitudo*

1 THIS say I therefore in the Lord,
        and testify to you,
   that henceforth ye no longer walk
        as other Gentiles do,

2 In vainness of their mind, whilst dark
        their understandings be,
   as those which from God's life estranged
        remain at enmity,

3 Through that gross ignorance in them
        that blindness doth impart,
   because of the confusion which
        doth lie upon their heart:

4 Who, past all feeling, give themselves
        unto licentiousness,
   that they may all uncleanness work,
        and that with greediness.

5 But ye have not so learned of Christ;
        if of him ye have heard,
   and, as the truth in Jesus is,
        have so been taught his word:

6 That ye concerning former things
        the old man put away,

EPHESIANS

    which after the deceitful lusts
      corrupt is found alway;

7 That in the spirit of your mind
    ye throughly be renewed;
and that the new man ye put on,
    with every grace endued;

8 Which, as created after God,
    doth even now appear
in righteousness and holiness,
    and in the truth sincere.

Hymn 74
Ephesians 5:1-5

Belmont

1 BE therefore followers of God,
    as children well belov'd;
and walk ye even as did Christ,
    who also hath us loved,

2 And given hath himself for us,
    an off'ring unto God,
a sacrifice that doth to him
    a savour sweet afford.

3 But fornication, uncleanness,
    or lusting wickedly,
among you, as becometh saints,
    let it not mentioned be:

4 Nay, neither filthiness, nor yet
    such words as fools do say,
nor jesting inconvenient:
    but give ye thanks alway.

5 For this ye know, no whoremonger,
   nor he that is unclean,
 nor one in heart idolatrous,
   which covetous hath been,

6 Hath part in that inheritance
   unto the heirs assured,
 of Christ's own kingdom glorious,
   and that which is of God.

Hymn 75

Ephesians 5:23, 25-27

Torwood

1 NOW of the church Christ is the head,
    and doth the body save:
 Christ loved the church, and for this cause
    himself he for it gave;

2 That he with water by the word
    might wash and cleanse the same,
 for, that it might be sanctified,
    in love he for it came:

3 That he a church most glorious
    unto himself might bring,
 without a wrinkle or a spot,
    or any suchlike thing;

4 That it without a blemish should
    in holiness abide,
 as nourished up and favoured well,
    an holy, heav'nly bride.

Hymn 76

Ephesians 6:10-11, 13-17

Martyrs

1 NOW in the Lord, and in his power,
    both strong and steadfast be;
  put on God's armour whole, and 'gainst
    the devil's wiles stand ye.

2 Take unto you God's armour whole,
    that in the evil day
  ye might withstand, and all things done,
    that stand indeed ye may.

3 Stand therefore, having girt about
    your loins with truthfulness,
  and having on the breastplate strong
    that is of righteousness;

4 And having on your feet that which
    shall you in safety bear,
  shod with the gospel of all peace
    which doth you well prepare;

5 Above all, take the shield of faith,
    which shall enable you
  to quench the wicked's fiery darts,
    and all of them subdue.

6 And take the helmet that to you
    salvation doth afford,
  and also take the Spirit's sword,
    which is the word of God.

HYMNS OF THE NEW TESTAMENT

HYMN 77
Philippians 1:9-11

Richmond

1 AND this I pray, that yet your love
   may more and more abound
 in knowledge and discernment clear,
   and in all judgment sound;

2 That those things which are excellent
   approve thereby may ye;
 that till the day of Christ ye might
   sincere and blameless be;

3 Filled with the fruits of righteousness
   by Jesus Christ always,
 that ye may render unto God
   the glory and the praise.

HYMN 78
Philippians 1:27-30

Caroline

1 LET all your conversation with
   Christ's gospel well agree;
 that I may of you hear, though I
   should come, or absent be:

2 That striving for the gospel's faith
   ye with one mind abide,
 and in one spirit; by your foes
   in nothing terrified:

3 Which of perdition evident
   a token doth afford

PHILIPPIANS

unto them all: but unto you
   salvation sent from God.

4 For in behalf of Christ, to you
    'tis given to partake
not only of belief in him,
   but suff'ring for his sake;

5 Whilst having that same conflict which
    in me at first ye saw,
and now do hear to be in me,
   a token true and sure.

Hymn 79
Philippians 2:5-11   *Vox Dilecti*

1 THIS mind, which in Christ Jesus was,
    let also in you be:
who, being in the form of God,
   abode in deity;

2 No robbery he did it think,
    no taking from his name,
that he himself as one with God
   equality should claim.

3 But of no reputation he
    himself spared not to make,
for of a servant he the form
   upon himself did take;

4 And in the likeness of mankind
    he made was to appear:
and being in man's fashion found,
   he unto men drew near.

5 Himself he humbled, yea, and though
    of all he suffered loss,
  to death became obedient,
    the death e'en of the cross.

6 Wherefore God also highly hath
    exalted him in love,
  and given him a name which is
    all other names above:

7 That every knee be made to bow
    at Jesus' holy name,
  of things in heaven, and in earth,
    and underneath the same;

8 And every tongue confess aloud
    that Jesus Christ is Lord,
  to God the Father glory that
    all creatures might afford.

Hymn 80

Philippians 2:12-16

S. Frances

1 BELOVED, as ye always have
    obeyed me heretofore,
  not only when I present am,
    but in my absence more,

2 Work ye your own salvation out,
    as is both meet and due,
  with fear and trembling evident
    in every one of you.

3 Because that it is God which doth
    work in you inwardly,

PHILIPPIANS

    that thereby of his pleasure good
      both will and do might ye.

4 Do all things without murmurings,
    disputings, or discord:
that wholly blameless ye may be,
    the harmless sons of God;

5 Those 'gainst whom there is no rebuke,
    although ye should be found
amidst a crooked nation where
    perverseness doth abound;

6 Among whom also in the world
    as lights ye shine abroad,
as one together holding forth
    of life the very word.

HYMN 81
Philippians 3:6-11   *Sheffield*

1 AS touching righteousness of law,
    though blameless found thereby,
the things that once were gain to me
    for Christ count loss did I.

2 Yea, doubtless, and I count all things
    as nothing to afford,
to gain the knowledge excellent
    of Christ Jesus my Lord:

3 For whom moreover of all things
    I suffered have the loss:
and, that I may win Christ, them all
    do count but dung and dross;

4 And that I might be found in him,
    not having as mine own
  the righteousness which to the law
    doth appertain alone;

5 But that which through the faith of Christ
    hath been by grace secured,
  that is, the righteousness of faith
    which is approved of God:

6 That I may know him, and the power
    by which raised up was he,
  that I his suff'rings' fellowship
    might know assuredly;

7 Not being made conformable
    unto his death in vain,
  if I the resurrection might
    by any means attain.

Hymn 82

Philippians 4:5-7

Evan

1 YOUR moderation in all things
      to all make known do ye;
  the Lord himself is near at hand:
    for nothing careful be.

2 But let in everything by prayer
    and supplication made
  with all thanksgiving, your requests
    be unto God conveyed.

COLOSSIANS

3 And so God's peace, which doth surpass
    all understanding deep,
 shall through Christ Jesus all your hearts
    and minds securely keep.

Hymn 83

Philippians 4:8 *Crimond*

1 NOW, brethren, whatsoever things
      there are of verity,
 what things soever honest are,
    or what things just that be;

2 Whatever things are pure, or what
      in loveliness are wrought,
 or whatsoever things ye hear
    that be of good report;

3 If there be any virtue found,
      if there be any praise,
 then meditate upon these things,
    and think on them always.

Hymn 84

Colossians 1:3-8 *Bedford*

1 WE render unfeigned thanks to God,
      and do the Father praise
 of our Lord Jesus Christ for you,
    for whom we pray always:

2 Since in Christ Jesus of your faith
      receive report did we,

and also of the love which show
  to all the saints do ye:

3 For that bless'd hope laid up for you,
    which is in heaven sure,
  taught in the word of gospel truth
    whereof ye heard before;

4 Which, as it is in all the world,
    is come unto you too;
  and bringeth forth its fruit, as it
    doth also bear in you,

5 Since ye it heard, and knew in truth
    the grace of God sincere;
  as of Epaphras ye did learn,
    our fellow-servant dear:

6 Who doth a faithful minister
    of Christ unto you prove,
  who also in the Spirit hath
    declared to us your love.

Hymn 85

Colossians 1:9-13 — *Newington*

1 WHEN first Epaphras of your love
      spake to us, since that day
  together for each one of you
      we do not cease to pray,

2 That with the knowledge of his will
      ye might indeed abound
  in understanding spiritual,
      and in all wisdom sound;

COLOSSIANS

3 That to all pleasing in the Lord
    your walk might worthy be,
and that ye might in each good work
    bear fruit abundantly,

4 Increasing in God's knowledge true,
    and with all might made strong,
by glorious pow'r, to patience all,
    with joy and suff'ring long;

5 Unto the Father giving thanks,
    for made us meet hath he,
that of the saints' inheritance
    in light partake should we:

6 Who from the pow'r of darkness hath
    delivered us each one,
and hath translated us into
    the realm of his dear Son.

HYMN 86

Colossians 1:13-17

Palestrina

1 INTO the realm of his dear Son
    translated us hath he,
in whom redemption through his blood
    together have do we,

2 That is, forgiveness of our sins:
    who is the image bright
of God which is invisible
    past all created sight;

3 The first-born of each creature found,
    who did all things create;
  who formed the creatures heavenly
    and earthly in estate;

4 Things visible, invisible,
    whatever thrones there be,
  or lordships, principals or powers:
    all things created he;

5 And for him they created were,
    by whom all things subsist;
  who is himself before all things,
    for by him they consist.

Hymn 87

Colossians 1:18-20

Lydia

1 HE of the body, e'en the church,
    exalted is as head:
  who also the beginning is,
    the first-born from the dead;

2 That greatly in pre-eminence
    he might o'er all excel;
  for it was pleasing that in him
    should all the fulness dwell:

3 And, through the blood of his own cross,
    peace having made on high,
  by him all things to reconcile
    and to himself make nigh;

4 By him, I say, of things in earth,
      whatever they might be,
   and likewise of all things above
      in places heavenly.

Hymn 88

Colossians 1:21-23

Lloyd

1 AND you, that sometime aliens
      and enemies were found
   within your mind by wicked works
      in which ye did abound,

2 He in the body of his flesh
      yet now hath reconciled
   through death, that you he might present
      both pure and undefiled:

3 Made holy and unblameable,
      and from offences free,
   before his sight: if in the faith
      continue still do ye,

4 As grounded, settled and unmoved,
      and holding fast the word
   that manifests the gospel hope,
      of which before ye heard:

5 Which was to all the creatures preached
      which 'neath the heavens be,
   whereof I Paul a minister
      am made in verity.

Hymn 89

Colossians 1:24-29

Kingsfold

1 I PAUL, in sufferings for you,
     rejoice with all goodwill,
   and fill up that which is behind
     of Christ's afflictions still,

2 Which in my flesh I gladly bear
     for his own body's sake,
   which is the church: whereof he did
     a minister me make,

3 According to the stewardship
     which God gave unto me,
   so that this selfsame word of God
     fulfilled in you might be;

4 The myst'ry e'en from ages hid,
     and generations past,
   but which is now made manifest
     unto his saints at last;

5 To whom among the Gentiles all
     God would make known to be
   the riches of the glory of
     the hidden mystery;

6 Which same is Christ in you, the hope
     of glory, whom we preach,
   and warn all men, as every man
     we in all wisdom teach;

7 That thereby every man present
     complete in him we may,

COLOSSIANS

as perfect in Christ Jesus found,
  and blameless in that day:

8 Whereunto also labour I
  and strive, as in his sight,
according to his working which
  doth work in me with might.

Hymn 90

Colossians 2:10-15   *Bishopthorpe*

1 YE are complete in him, who is
  raised up from death again,
who o'er all principality
  and pow'r as head doth reign.

2 For in him ye are circumcised
  by that made without hands,
in putting off the body which
  in sinful nature stands,

3 By circumcision wrought in Christ:
  for when baptised were ye,
ye buried with him were, wherein
  ye risen with him be,

4 Raised through the faith of that which is
  God's operation sure,
who hath him raised up from the dead
  to live for evermore.

5 And you, dead in your sins, in flesh
  uncircumcised which be,
as one together bound with him,
  made quick and live hath he,

6 Forgiving you all trespasses;
   and blotting out withal
the handwriting of ord'nances
   that was against us all,

7 Which unto us was contrary
   and over us prevailed,
and took the same out of the way
   and to his cross it nailed;

8 For spoiling principalities,
   and bringing pow'rs to loss,
he made an open show of them,
   triumphing in the cross.

Hymn 91

Colossians 3:1-4

Tiverton

1 IF then ye risen be with Christ,
      the things above seek ye,
   where Christ upon God's own right hand
      doth sit triumphantly.

2 On high set your affection, not
      on things on earth that be:
   with Christ in God your life is hid,
      and dead with him are ye.

3 When Christ, who is our life above,
      shall at the last draw near,
   then in his glory raised with him
      ye also shall appear.

Hymn 92

Colossians 3:5-11

Grafton

1 YOUR members therefore mortify
　　upon the earth do ye;
both fornication and its lust,
　　with things unclean that be,

2 Affections most inordinate,
　　diverse iniquity,
and every form of coveting,
　　which is idolatry:

3 For which things' sake the wrath of God
　　shall come in that great day
upon the children that are born
　　of those that disobey:

4 In which ye sometime walked and lived.
　　But now each one do ye
put off such things as anger, wrath,
　　malice and blasphemy,

5 And filthy conversation all,
　　that from your mouth doth sound.
To one another lie no more,
　　nor in deceit be found.

6 Because the old man with his deeds
　　put off from you have ye,
and have the new man now put on
　　in truth and verity;

7 Which is renewed in knowledge true,
　　and heavenly estate,

after the image of the one
   that did the same create:
8 Where there is neither Greek nor Jew,
   nor bond, nor free withal,
nor circumcision, nation, but
   where Christ is all in all.

Hymn 93

Colossians 3:12-17

Westminster

1 AS loved and holy, God's elect,
      do ye unto you bind
   the bowels of mercies, kindness mild,
      and humbleness of mind;

2 With meekness and long-suffering,
      forbearance exercise;
   let each forgive the other one
      if quarrels should arise:

3 As Christ forgave you, so do ye
      to those that you transgress.
   Above all put on charity,
      the bond of perfectness.

4 And let God's peace rule in your hearts,
      unto the which are ye
   together in one body called;
      and thankful also be.

5 Let richly in all wisdom dwell
      the word of Christ in you;
   both teaching and admonishing
      each one with doctrine true;

6 In psalms and hymns and holy songs,
    most spiritual that be,
as in your hearts unto the Lord
    sing forth with grace do ye.

7 Do all ye do in word or deed
    in the Lord Jesus' name,
to God and to the Father thanks
    expressing in the same.

Hymn 94

I Thessalonians 1:2-8

Martyrdom

1 WE always unto God give thanks
    and mention of you make
in prayers and intercessions which
    we offer for your sake;

2 Rememb'ring ceaselessly your work
    of faith, and toil of love,
and patient hope set in the Lord,
    e'en Jesus Christ above,

3 In God and in our Father's sight;
    as knowing, brethren true,
that by election in his love
    God hath made choice of you.

4 Because our gospel to you all
    came not in word alone:
but in the Holy Ghost and power,
    with much assurance shown.

HYMNS OF THE NEW TESTAMENT

5 Ye know among you for your sake
    what kind of men were we.
And straightway followers of us
    and of the Lord were ye;

6 As having in affliction great
    the word with joy received
and gladness of the Holy Ghost,
    when ye at first believed:

7 Yea, ye examples were to all
    believers found abroad,
for from you sounded out the word
    that cometh from the Lord.

Hymn 95

I Thessalonians 1:8-10

Invocation

1 YOUR faith to Godward in each place
    by all abroad is spread,
so that we nothing need to speak
    that is not by them said:

2 Because they of themselves do tell
    the manner that was shown
by us when ent'ring in to you
    to make our gospel known:

3 How unto God from idols false
    turn at our word did ye,
that of the living God and true
    the servants ye might be:

I THESSALONIANS

4 His Son from heaven to await,
 whom raise from death did he,
e'en Jesus, from the wrath to come
 who saved and set us free.

Hymn 96

I Thessalonians 2:2-5

Belmont

1 BUT after we had suffered much,
 and treated were with shame,
 we bold were in our God to you
 to preach that worthy name.

2 For that we with contention great
 God's gospel did proclaim:
 yea, unto you without deceit
 our exhortation came;

3 Not of uncleanness, nor in guile:
 but as allowed were we
 entrusted with the gospel truth
 of God himself to be,

4 So speak we; not as pleasing men,
 but God, our hearts which tries.
 For we at no time used false words,
 nor flattered men with lies;

5 Nor did we covetousness cloak,
 as ye are all aware;
 nor did we glory seek from men,
 as God doth witness bear.

HYMN 97

I Thessalonians 2:13-16

Barrow

1 FOR this cause always thank we God,
   because when ye received
the word of God from us, 'twas not
   men's word that ye believed;

2 But, as it is in truth, God's word,
   effectively inwrought
in you together that by faith
   believe what we have taught.

3 For of God's churches 'midst the Jews,
   which in Christ Jesus be,
ye followers became, in that
   the like things suffered ye

4 Of your own countrymen, as they
   did also of the Jews:
who the Lord Jesus killed, and who
   their prophets did abuse;

5 And they have persecuted us:
   and God they do not please.
Besides this, even contrary
   unto all men are these.

6 And lest the Gentiles should be saved,
   forbid they us to speak;
as fully knowing that in truth
   we their salvation seek.

I THESSALONIANS

7 For alway they their sins fill up,
   that in the law do boast.
  Behold, the wrath is come on them
   unto the uttermost.

HYMN 98

I Thessalonians 4:13-17

There is a Fountain + refrain

1 I WOULD not have you ignorant
   concerning them which sleep,
  that ye, as others without hope,
   should sorrow not nor weep.

2 If we believe that Jesus died,
   and rose from death anew,
  then them which do in Jesus sleep
   will God bring with him too.

3 We by the Lord's word say that we
   which yet alive remain
  shall not prevent them which do sleep,
   when comes the Lord again.

4 For with a shout the Lord himself
   descend from heaven shall,
  with the archangel's voice, and with
   God's final trumpet call.

5 And first the dead in Christ shall rise:
   and then together we,
  which yet alive are, in the clouds
   caught up with them shall be;

6 So that the Lord we in the air
   might meet with one accord;
  and so we shall together be
   for ever with the Lord.

Hymn 99

II Thessalonians 1:3-10

Old 81st

1 To thank God, brethren, as is meet,
   we constantly are bound,
  for your faith's growth, and for the love
   which in you doth abound.

2 For in God's churches all our boast
   is of your patience sure,
  your faith in persecutions, yea,
   and trials that ye endure;

3 Which of God's judgment righteous is
   a token all may see,
  that worthy ye that suffer ill
   might of God's kingdom be:

4 Since unto them that trouble you
   it is a righteous thing
  that God should recompense your grief,
   and judgment on them bring.

5 But in your trouble rest with us,
   when be revealed there shall
  from heaven the Lord Jesus with
   his mighty angels all,

II THESSALONIANS

6 With vengeance wrought in flaming fire
  on them that know not God,
and that of our Lord Jesus Christ
  the gospel have abhorred:

7 Whom with eternal punishment
  destruction shall devour,
sent from the presence of the Lord,
  and glory of his power;

8 When he shall come, that in his saints
  he glorified should be,
and in all them that do believe
  admired exceedingly.

Hymn 100
II Thessalonians 2:3-4, 6-12

Old 22nd

1 BY no means let one you deceive
    concerning that great day:
  for first comes an apostasy,
    when many fall away.

2 And then perdition's son, the man
    of sin, shall be exposed,
  becoming, over all named God,
    exalted and opposed;

3 Himself to lift o'er that on which
    men worship do bestow;
  so that he in God's temple sits,
    himself as God to show.

HYMNS OF THE NEW TESTAMENT

4 And now ye know what doth withhold,
    and what is yet concealed,
until the time appointed comes,
    when he shall be revealed.

5 Already of iniquity
    doth work the mystery:
but he that hinders, hinder will,
    until he taken be.

6 Then shall that Wicked be revealed,
    he whom the Lord shall smite
with his mouth's spirit, and destroy
    with his own coming bright:

7 E'en him who, after Satan's work,
    himself doth magnify,
as coming with all pow'r, and signs,
    and wonders that do lie;

8 With all unrighteousness' deceit
    in them that lost shall be;
who, to be saved, would not receive
    the truth in charity.

9 And for this cause shall God himself
    unto them from on high
a strong delusion send, by which
    they should believe a lie:

10 That they might all be damned, the truth
    who neither would confess
nor yet believe, but pleasure took
    in their unrighteousness.

Hymn 101
II Thessalonians 2:13-17

Harington

1 BUT we are bound to render thanks
    unceasingly to God,
on your behalf, our brethren dear,
    beloved of the Lord:

2 For God afore hath chosen you
    unto salvation free,
that, by the Spirit sanctified,
    believe the truth should ye;

3 Whence you he by that gospel called
    which doth to us pertain,
that ye of our Lord Jesus Christ
    the glory might obtain.

4 Stand fast, and the traditions hold
    which unto you we brought;
yea, brethren, whether 'twere by word,
    or by our letters taught.

5 Now our Lord Jesus Christ himself,
    and God, our Father, too,
in love who ever gave to us
    a consolation true,

6 Yea, and withal good hope through grace:
    your hearts with comfort stay,
and in each goodly word and work
    establish you alway.

HYMN 102
I Timothy 1:(1-3) 4-11

Gloucester

1 I PAUL, as in mine absence long,
      thee, Timothy, beseech
   that some thou mightest charge that they
      no other doctrine teach;

2 And neither heed to fables give
      which do but gender lies,
   and endless genealogies
      which questions cause to rise;

3 But godly edifying which
      doth faith itself impart.
   Now of the charge the end is love
      which comes from a pure heart,

4 And of a conscience that is good,
      and faith that none can feign:
   from which some, having swerved aside,
      have turned to jangling vain;

5 For these are they which do desire
      that teachers they should be
   e'en of the law they neither know
      nor teach in verity;

6 Who understand not what they say,
      nor whereof they affirm.
   But that the lawful use of law
      is good, we do confirm:

I TIMOTHY

7 Not being for a just man made,
    but for those lawless found,
  for all the disobedient
    and godless that abound,

8 For sinners and unholy men,
    that speak profanity,
  for such as take their parents' lives,
    for all that slayers be,

9 For whoremongers and sodomites,
    for those that men do steal,
  for liars, perjured persons, and
    for those that falsely deal,

10 Against the doctrine that is taught
    according to the word,
  e'en of the gospel glorious
    sent of the blessed God.

Hymn 103
1 Timothy 1:15-17

Nativity

1 THIS faithful saying worthy is,
    of all received to be:
  Christ Jesus came into the world
    that sinners save might he;

2 Of whom, saith Paul, I am the chief:
    but mercy I was shown
  that Jesus Christ might in me first
    all suff'ring long make known:

3 That this a pattern should set forth
    for all them to receive
  which to eternal life on him
    hereafter should believe.

4 Now unto the eternal King
    let praise for ever rise;
  immortal and invisible,
    to God the only wise:

5 Yea, honour great and glory be,
    for ever to endure,
  from this time forth to ages all,
    Amen, for evermore.

Hymn 104

I Timothy 2:1-6

Crediton

1 THAT supplications, prayers, be made,
    I first of all entreat,
  with intercessions, giving thanks,
    for all men, as is meet;

2 For kings, all in authority:
    that lead in peace may we
  a life of quiet godliness
    and unfeigned honesty.

3 This good is and acceptable
    in God our Saviour's sight,
  who will have all men to be saved,
    and know the truth aright.

I TIMOTHY

4 For there one God is, and therewith
    the mediator one,
the man Christ Jesus, who doth stand
    'twixt God and men alone;

5 Who gave himself, that he for all
    a ransom might provide;
for he it is that in due time
    is to be testified.

Hymn 105
I Timothy 2:7-15

S. Peter

1 I, PAUL, a preacher am ordained,
    and an apostle true,
(in this I speak the truth in Christ,
    and lie not unto you;)

2 A teacher of the Gentiles all,
    in faith and verity.
I will that therefore everywhere
    men pray continually,

3 As without wrath or doubting, but
    with holy hands upborne.
That women likewise should themselves
    in comely dress adorn;

4 With modesty and soberness,
    and not with broided hair,
or gold, or pearls, or costly things
    of an appearance fair;

5 But (as it women doth become
      professing godliness)
   let them adorned be with good works
      of proper comeliness.

6 In silence let the woman learn
      with all subjection meek.
   But I a woman suffer not
      in teaching e'er to speak,

7 Nor to usurp authority
      or rise above man's place,
   but to be found in silence, and
      behave with shame of face.

8 For first was Adam formed, then Eve.
      The man was not deceived:
   but Eve in the transgression was,
      for she the lie believed.

9 But notwithstanding she shall be
      through that child-bearing saved;
   if they in faith, love, holiness,
      are soberly behaved.

Hymn 106
I Timothy 3:14-16

Westminster

1 LEST I should tarry long, these things
      I written to thee have,
   that thou may'st know how in God's house
      thou oughtest to behave:

I TIMOTHY

2 Because it is the church in which
    the living God is found,
and which is both the pillar, yea,
    and of the truth the ground.

3 And this I unto thee declare
    without controversy,
pertaining unto godliness,
    great is the mystery:

4 Because that truly in the flesh
    God manifest hath been,
yea, in the Spirit justified,
    and so of angels seen;

5 And to the Gentiles preached in turn,
    and in the world believed,
then into glory, at the last,
    assuredly received.

Hymn 107
I Timothy 4:1-6

S. Flavian

1 THE Spirit doth expressly speak
    this warning unto all,
that in the last times from the faith
    some shall depart and fall;

2 Heed giving unto spirits that
    base and seducing be,
and devils' doctrines, speaking lies
    in their hypocrisy;

3 Their conscience being seared and burned
    as with an iron hot;
  commanding to abstain from things
    which God commanded not.

4 Each thing that God hath made is good,
    and will not men ensnare,
  if it with thanks be sanctified
    by God's own word and prayer.

5 If thou the brethren to these things
    recall, and be not moved,
  then thou a minister shalt be
    of Jesus Christ approved:

6 In words of faith, and doctrine good,
    both nourished and sustained,
  whereunto also even now
    thou hast indeed attained.

Hymn 108
I Timothy 4:11-16

S. James

1 THESE things command and teach: let none
    despise thy tender youth;
  but be thou an example sound
    to all that hold the truth:

2 In word, in conversation, and
    in fervent charity,
  in spirit, and in faith unfeigned,
    and inward purity.

I TIMOTHY

3 Until I come, attendance give
    to reading holy truth,
to exhortation, doctrine sound;
    be sparing of reproof.

4 The gift in thee neglect thou not,
    which given was to thee
by prophecy, with laid-on hands
    of all the presbyt'ry.

5 Upon these things oft meditate,
    whole-hearted and sincere;
thyself give to them, that to all
    thy profit may appear.

6 Unto thyself take constant heed,
    and to the doctrine true:
in doing this thou'lt save thyself,
    and them that hear thee too.

Hymn 109
I Timothy 6:14-16

Effingham

1 KEEP this commandment without spot,
    as from all blemish clear,
till our Lord Jesus Christ himself
    shall in that day appear:

2 The bless'd and only Potentate,
    the King of kings is he,
and Lord of lords, whose times declare
    sole immortality;

Hymn 110
II Timothy 1:9-11

Bishopthorpe

1 GOD hath us saved, and us by grace
   called with an holy call,
not wrought according to our works,
   nor of ourselves at all,

2 But after his own purpose which,
   through grace abundantly,
was in Christ Jesus given us
   ere form the world did he;

3 But which by the appearing hath
   been now made manifest,
by that same grace which Jesus Christ
   our Saviour hath expressed;

4 Who hath abolished death itself,
   and brought triumphantly
through his own gospel life to light,
   and immortality:

[Previous hymn, verses 3-4:]

3 In light which cannot be approached
   hid from the sight of man;
whom no man ever hath beheld,
   and no man ever can:

4 To whom the honour glorious
   doth only appertain,
with everlasting might and power.
   Amen, yea, and Amen.

II TIMOTHY

5 Whereunto I appointed am
    this mystery to preach,
and sent forth an apostle, called
    the Gentiles for to teach.

HYMN 111
II Timothy 2:8-15

S. Matthew

1 DO thou remember that which I
    have in my gospel said,
that Jesus Christ, of David's seed,
    was raised up from the dead:

2 Wherein, as one that doeth ill,
    I am in trouble found,
yea, even unto bonds: but still
    God's word cannot be bound.

3 All things for the elect I bear,
    so that salvation sure
they in Christ Jesus may obtain
    with glory evermore.

4 For it a faithful saying is:
    If dead with him we be,
then it shall surely come to pass
    that live with him shall we;

5 And if we suffer, we in turn
    shall also with him reign;
and if we him deny, then he
    will us deny again;

6 If we believe not, nonetheless
   he faithful doth abide;
for he cannot at any time
   be by himself denied.

7 These things repeat: before the Lord
   give charge that all may fear,
and strive not with words profitless,
   subverting those that hear.

8 To show thyself approved of God
   in study be unblamed:
divide the word of truth aright,
   a workman unashamed.

Hymn 112
II Timothy 3:1-6, 8-9

Old 81st

1 THIS know, that in the latter days,
      when near the end shall be,
   times that are yet more perilous
      shall come with certainty.

2 Men shall be lovers of themselves,
      and covetous alway;
   vain boasters, proud, blasphemers, who
      their parents disobey,

3 Unthankful and unholy, void
      of all affection kind,
   truce-breakers, false accusers, and
      incontinent of mind,

II TIMOTHY

4 Fierce, and despisers of the good,
   ill traitors, heady all,
high-minded, who their pleasures love
   more than their God withal;

5 Who do a form of godliness
   in outward things display,
but who deny the pow'r thereof:
   from such turn thou away.

6 This sort do into houses creep,
   and silly women lead
as captives, laden with their sins,
   and lusts diverse indeed.

7 As Jannes and Jambres Moses scorned,
   the truth these disobey:
corrupt in mind, and reprobate
   concerning faith are they.

8 But they no further shall proceed:
   for manifest shall be
their folly unto all, as once
   men also theirs did see.

Hymn 113

II Timothy 3:10-13

Lynton

1 THOU hast my doctrine fully known,
      of life my manner too;
   the purpose, faith, long-suff'ring, love,
      and patience I pursue:

2 My persecutions, too, thou'st known,
    and the afflictions all
at Antioch, Iconium,
    which did upon me fall;

3 What trials and persecutions great
    at Lystra suffered I:
but from them all the Lord did me
    deliver by and by.

4 Yea, and all in Christ Jesus that
    live lives of godliness,
shall suffer persecution which
    shall oft-times them oppress.

5 But evil and seducing men
    shall worse and worse become,
deceiving others, whilst they are
    of lies themselves o'ercome.

Hymn 114
II Timothy 3:14-17

Arnold

1 CONTINUE thou in those things which
    thou hast in me discerned,
and been assured of, knowing well
    of whom thou hast them learned;

2 And that thou from thy childhood hast
    the holy scriptures known,
to make thee to salvation wise
    which able are alone;

II TIMOTHY

3 Through faith which in Christ Jesus hath
     been unto thee assured.
  Because all scripture is inspired
     and breathed upon by God;

4 And doth for doctrine profit much,
     and likewise for reproof,
  both to correct and to instruct
     in righteousness and truth:

5 That so the man of God may be
     made perfect, as is meet,
  and throughly unto all good works
     well furnished and complete.

Hymn 115
II Timothy 4:2-5
Beatitudo

1 THE word preach, instant at all times,
      as thou'st of me been taught;
  with doctrine, and long-suffering,
      reprove, rebuke, exhort.

2 The time will come when they will not
     endure such doctrine sound,
  but walk shall after their own lusts
     which greatly shall abound:

3 Then shall they to themselves heap men
     that preach without reproof,
  with itching ears; and so they shall
     their ears turn from the truth;

4 And shall be unto fables turned.
   Take heed, O man of God!
do thou a watch in all things keep;
   bear thou affliction's rod.

5 Of an evangelist do thou
   unto the work attend;
yea, make thou of thy ministry
   full proof unto the end.

HYMN 116
II Timothy 4:6-8

Spohr

1 THAT I might now be offered up,
   I, Paul, do ready stand:
of my departure from this world
   the time is nigh at hand.

2 I have a good fight fought, as thou
   of me canst testify,
I likewise finished have my course,
   and kept the faith have I.

3 Henceforth there is laid up for me
   a crown of righteousness,
which from the Lord, the just judge, I
   shall in that day possess.

4 Now know I therefore that my crown
   reserved is far above,
and not for me alone, but all
   that his appearing love.

HYMN 117

Titus 1:1-4

Bedford

1 GOD'S servant, an apostle sent
   of Jesus Christ, named Paul;
 according to the faith by which
   God his elect doth call:

2 And also the acknowledging,
   in steadfast faithfulness,
 of that same truth, which in itself
   is after godliness;

3 In hope of everlasting life,
   which God, that cannot lie,
 did promise, ere he made the earth,
   or formed the heavens high;

4 But manifested hath in time
   his word abundantly
 through preaching of the truth, which is
   committed unto me,

5 According to that which hath been
   commanded and assured,
 of him that unto us is made
   our Saviour and our God:

6 To Titus, called, a minister,
   sent forth from him above,
 according to the common faith,
   as mine own son in love:

7 Grace, mercy, peace, be unto thee,
   from God the Father shown,
and the Lord Jesus Christ, who is
   to us as Saviour known.

Hymn 118
Titus 2:11-15

Noel

1 THE grace of God which unto us
     doth true salvation bring,
appeared hath unto every man,
   us all admonishing,

2 That we, denying godlessness,
   and every worldly lust,
should soberly and righteously
   live godly lives and just;

3 Whilst in this world we look for that
   bless'd hope which draweth near,
when the great God and Jesus Christ
   our Saviour shall appear:

4 Who gave himself an offering
   that he might set us free,
redeeming and deliv'ring us
   from all iniquity;

5 So that a people purify
   unto himself might he,
peculiar, that of good works
   exceeding zealous be.

6 These things with boldness do thou speak,
    exhort in any wise,
rebuke with all authority.
    Let no man thee despise.

Hymn 119
Titus 3:3-7

Sheffield

1 WE sometimes foolish were ourselves,
      as those that disobey,
  deceived, and serving divers lusts
      and pleasures every day;

2 In malice living all the while,
      and envy constantly,
  both hateful, and to everyone
      behaving hatefully.

3 But nonetheless 'twas after that
      the kindness and the love
  of God our Saviour unto man
      revealed was from above.

4 'Twas not by works of righteousness
      which we ourselves had wrought,
  but after his own mercy he
      to us salvation brought,

5 By that regeneration which
      by washing we obtain,
  and that renewing which doth to
      the Holy Ghost pertain;

6 Which he upon us from above
    shed forth abundantly,
through Jesus Christ whom unto us
    as Saviour send did he;

7 That by his grace now justified,
    be counted heirs should we,
according to the hope of life
    that shall eternal be.

Hymn 120

Philemon 4-7, 25

S. Stephen

1 I RENDER thanks unto my God,
    and mention of thee make
continually in all the prayers
    I offer for thy sake;

2 On hearing of thy love and faith,
    which were to me made known,
which thou to the Lord Jesus hast,
    and to the saints each one:

3 That so the sharing of thy faith
    effectual might be,
by owning in Christ Jesus each
    good thing that is in thee.

4 For we have consolation great,
    and joy sent from above,
because the bowels of the saints
    refreshed are by thy love.

Hymn 121

Hebrews 1:1-3

Ballerma

1 GOD, who afore at sundry times
   in divers manners spake
unto the fathers by all those
   whom he did prophets make,

2 Hath in these last times by his Son
   his speech to us conveyed,
whom he appointed hath the heir
   of all things that are made,

3 By whom he also made the worlds
   to form at his behest;
who being of his glory great
   the brightness manifest,

4 And being of the image true,
   and character express,
of him who in his person doth
   full deity possess,

5 And all things by his word of power
   upholding in his might,
when he our sins had by himself
   purged throughly from his sight,

6 Sat down in places heavenly,
       made to the right hand nigh
   of that exalted Majesty
       enthroned in heaven high.

Hymn 122
Hebrews 1:5-9

Stroudwater

1 FOR of the angels unto which
       at any time said he,
   Thou art mine only Son, this day
       have I begotten thee?

2 As he again doth say, To him
       a Father I will be,
   and he shall be to me a Son?
       As once again saith he,

3 When he into the world doth bring
       the first-begotten one,
   Let all God's angels magnify
       and worship him alone.

4 And of the angels he doth say,
       Who hath as spirits made
   his angels, and in flames of fire
       his ministers arrayed.

5 But to the Son 'tis otherwise,
       for unto him saith he,
   Thy throne, O God, hath ever been,
       and evermore shall be:

HEBREWS

6 The sceptre of thy kingdom just
    is one of righteousness.
Thou righteousness hast always loved,
    and hated lawlessness;

7 And therefore God, thy God himself,
    hath e'en anointed thee
with oil of gladness far above
    thy fellows all that be.

Hymn 123

Hebrews 1:10-14

Coleshill

1 THOU, Lord, in the beginning hast
    the earth's foundation laid,
yea, and the very heavens thou
    by thine own hands hast made:

2 They perish shall, but thou remain'st;
    yea, they shall all wax old
as doth a garment; and thou shalt
    them as a vesture fold.

3 And they shall all be changed: but thou
    art evermore the same,
thy years shall neither fade nor fail,
    enduring is thy name.

4 But of the angels unto which
    at any time said he,
Sit on my right, till I thy foes
    thy footstool make to be?

Hymn 124

Hebrews 2:1-4

Elgin

1. WE ought to give more earnest heed
    to those things held which be,
   lest let them slip through negligence
    at any time should we.

2. For if the word was steadfast which
    the angels spake before,
   so that the least transgression wrought
    against that holy law,

3. And likewise also every form
    of disobedience,
   received as just and sure reward
    the strictest recompense:

4. Then how shall we ourselves escape,
    if we should now the more
   neglect so great salvation, which
    by far transcends the law;

5. In which the Lord himself at first
    began to speak the word,
   and which was unto us confirmed
    by those that had him heard:

6 With wondrous signs and miracles
   God to them witnessing,
 and gifts which in his will to them
   the Holy Ghost did bring?

Hymn 125
Hebrews 2:11-15

Irish

1 FOR both he that through sufferings
      doth sanctify his own,
  and they who have been sanctified,
      alike are all of one.

2 For which cause brethren them to call
      doth bring to him no shame,
  I to my brethren will, saith he,
      declare thy holy name;

3 And also I amidst the church
      will praise sing unto thee.
  He saith again, In him alone
      my trust shall ever be.

4 And yet again he saith, Behold
      I and the children dear
  which God hath given unto me,
      one with me to appear.

5 For as the children all partake
      of flesh and blood, so he
  did of the same take part: that thus
      he might the children free;

6 That him that had the pow'r of death
   he might of pow'r make void,
that is, the devil, so that he
   through death might be destroyed;

7 And them deliver who through fear
   of death their lifetime long
each day to bondage subject were,
   and to oppression strong.

Hymn 126
Hebrews 3:12-19

Abney

1 TAKE heed, lest there in any one
      be found an evil heart
of unbelief, that ye should from
   the living God depart.

2 But daily, while 'tis called Today,
   each one exhort do ye;
lest any through deceitfulness
   of sin should hardened be.

3 For true partakers we of Christ
   are made, if we extend
the confidence we held at first
   steadfast unto the end;

4 While it to us is said, Today
   if hear his voice ye will,
then harden not your hearts, as in
   the provocation ill.

5 For some, when they had heard, provoked:
    howbeit not the sum
  of those that out of Egypt's land
    by Moses' hand did come.

6 But who did grieve him forty years?
    was it indeed not all
  that sinned, within the wilderness
    whose carcasses did fall?

7 And unto whom sware he that they
    should to his rest not come,
  but unto them through unbelief
    that hardened had become?

8 So see we from the scripture that
    they could not enter in,
  but perished in the wilderness
    through unbelief and sin.

Hymn 127
Hebrews 4:7, 9-13

Hermon

1 TODAY if ye will hear his voice,
    your hearts do not make hard:
  for there a rest remains unto
    the people called of God.

2 For he that into promised rest
    most surely entered is
  hath also ceased from his own works,
    as God did first from his.

3 Then let us therefore labour still
   that rest to enter in,
 lest we as those that were of old
   through unbelief should sin.

4 Because that quick and powerful
   abides the word of God,
 and also doth more sharply cut
   than any two-edged sword;

5 As piercing to divide the soul
   and spirit e'en in twain,
 besides the joints and marrow that
   doth to the same pertain;

6 And a discerner is withal
   to tell the thoughts apart
 from the intentions that do lie
   concealed within the heart.

7 Nor is there any creature found
   that is not in his view:
 but all is open to his eyes
   with whom we have to do.

Hymn 128

Hebrews 4:14-16

Psalm 107

1 THEN, since we have a great high priest
      into the heavens passed,
 Jesus the Son of God, let us
   hold our profession fast.

HEBREWS

2 For we an high priest do not have
    our need that never sees,
nor with the feeling is untouched
    of our infirmities;

3 But was in all points tempted sore
    as we, yet without sin.
Then let us therefore by him come,
    and boldly enter in,

4 So that before the throne of grace
    we mercy may obtain,
and find the grace in time of need
    that will our hearts sustain.

Hymn 129

Hebrews 5:5-10

Morven

1 CHRIST did not glorify himself
    a great high priest to be;
but he that said, Thou art my Son,
    this day begat I thee.

2 As also in another place,
    Thou art a priest, saith he,
in order like Melchisedec,
    for evermore to be.

3 Who in the past days of his flesh,
    what time that he had prayed,
and had with crying strong, and tears,
    his supplications made,

HYMNS OF THE NEW TESTAMENT

4 To him that able was from death
   to save and set him free,
and for his piety was heard,
   in that him fear did he;

5 Although he were a Son, yet he
   obedience learned still
by all the things he suffered in
   submission to his will;

6 And as perfected, to all them
   that him obey was he
the author of salvation made
   unto eternity;

7 Of God called an high priest, who him
   to priesthood did ordain
after the order which doth to
   Melchisedec pertain.

Hymn 130
Hebrews 6:4-9

Dalehurst

1 IT is impossible for those
   who did at first repent
and were enlightened, and did taste
   the gift from heaven sent,

2 And of the Holy Ghost partook,
   and God's good word did taste,
and of the world that is to come
   the heav'nly pow'rs embraced,

3 If they shall fall, to penitence
    again them to renew;
  for to themselves they crucify
    the Son of God anew;

4 And him to open shame they put.
    For earth which drinketh rain
  to bring forth herbs for them that plant
    God's blessing doth retain:

5 But that which beareth thorns and briers
    by them that plant is spurned,
  and of them is to cursing nigh,
    whose end is to be burned.

6 But better things of you, belov'd,
    persuaded yet are we,
  and things salvation that attend,
    though thus our speech should be.

Hymn 131
Hebrews 6:13-18

Bangor

1 WHEN God first unto Abraham
    his promise did declare,
  because there was none greater found,
    he by himself did swear,

2 Declaring, Thee in blessing bless
    assuredly will I,
  and likewise multiplying thee,
    I will thee multiply.

HYMNS OF THE NEW TESTAMENT

3 And so, when it had come to pass
    that Abr'ham patiently
had all things borne, the promised vow
    obtain from him did he.

4 For men do by the greater swear,
    and do an oath commend
as confirmation that all strife
    is brought unto an end.

5 Wherein God, more abundantly
    found willing to display
the sure immutability
    that in his counsel lay,

6 Confirmed it by an oath to those
    that heirs of promise be:
that by two things immutable,
    affirmed in verity,

7 In which it was impossible
    that God should ever lie,
we might a consolation have,
    and strength obtain thereby.

Hymn 132

Hebrews 6:18-20

Nativity

1 WE have a consolation strong
    who do for refuge flee
to lay hold on the sure hope which
    before us set hath he;

2 Which hope we as an anchor have
    that doth the soul avail,
both sure and steadfast, ent'ring in
    to that within the veil:

3 Where Jesus our forerunner great
    is entered in before,
made like unto Melchisedec,
    an high priest evermore.

Hymn 133
Hebrews 7:21-25

Vox Dilecti

1 THE Lord hath sworn, nor will repent,
      For evermore thou art
a priest like to Melchisedec,
    in order set apart.

2 For by so much a surety
    was Jesus made before
of that much better testament
    which stablished is and sure.

3 And truly they were many priests,
    as also scripture saith,
which were not suffered to remain
    by reason of their death:

4 But this one man, because that he
    continues evermore,
a priesthood hath unchangeable
    that ever shall endure.

5 Wherefore he able also is
    salvation to afford
unto the uttermost to them
    that come by him to God;

6 Yea, seeing that he ever lives
    for them to intercede,
who died for them and rose on high,
    on their behalf to plead.

Hymn 134

Hebrews 7:26 - 8:3

S. David

1 SUCH an high priest became us, who
    is holy, harmless, pure,
apart from sinners, made above
    the very heavens sure:

2 Who needeth not, as those high priests,
    to offer each day new
a sacrifice, first for his sins,
    then for the people's too:

3 For when he offered up himself,
    this once for all did he.
For Moses' law makes men high priests
    which have infirmity;

4 But that word given by the oath,
    and spoken since the law,
doth make the consecrated Son
    a priest for evermore.

HEBREWS

5 Now of these things this is the sum:
    Such an high priest have we
set on the right hand of the throne
    of heav'nly Majesty;

6 A minister of holy things,
    in holy places new:
that which the Lord, not man, did pitch,
    the tabernacle true.

7 For those high priests made off'rings which
    were for that time ordained,
but this man offered once that which
    perfection hath obtained.

Hymn 135

Hebrews 8:6-9

Caithness

1 A MINISTRY more excellent
    obtained of him hath he,
that of a cov'nant new he might
    the mediator be;

2 Which covenant established is,
    for ever to endure,
upon those better promises
    which certain are and sure.

3 For had that cov'nant faultless been
    which had to them been taught,
then for the second there had been
    no place thereafter sought.

HYMNS OF THE NEW TESTAMENT

4 For finding fault with them, he saith,
Behold, the days are nigh,
thus saith the Lord, when make with them
a cov'nant new will I,

5 With Isr'el's and with Judah's house:
not like that which I made
in that day with their fathers, when
hold on their hand I laid,

6 To lead them out of Egypt's land;
because that they abhorred
my covenant, and them I did
regard not, saith the Lord.

Hymn 136

Hebrews 8:10-13

Harington

1 BEHOLD, this is the covenant,
which, saith the Lord most high,
make with the house of Israel
after those days will I:

2 My laws I in their mind will put,
and in their hearts them write:
I'll be their God, and they shall be
a people in my sight:

3 His neighbour each man shall not teach,
nor each his brother tell,
The Lord know: for both small and great
alike shall know me well.

4 For unto their unrighteousness
    be merciful I shall;
  their sins and their iniquities
    I will no more recall.

5 In that he saith, A new, he hath
    the first made to decay.
  That which doth perish and wax old
    shall vanish soon away.

Hymn 137

Hebrews 9:1-5

Tallis

1 THAT cov'nant which was first decreed
      had also verily
  its ordinance of service, and
      a worldly sanctuary.

2 For there a tabernacle was:
      the first, which did embrace
  the candlestick and table with
      the shewbread set in place;

3 This is the sanctuary. And next
      the second veil doth fall,
  and then the tabernacle called
      the Holiest of all;

4 Wherein the golden censer was,
      and where to rest was laid
  the ark of that first covenant,
      with gold all overlaid;

5 In which was found the golden pot
    that manna did contain,
  and Aaron's rod that budded, and
    the cov'nant tables twain;

6 And over it the cherubims
    to glory that pertained,
  o'ershadowing the mercy-seat
    which was of him ordained.

Hymn 138

Hebrews 9:6-10

S. Fulbert

1 NOW when the law had been ordained,
    the priests did go at will
  into the tabernacle first,
    their service to fulfil.

2 But in the tabernacle next
    the high priest went alone
  once every year, not without blood
    which did for sin atone;

3 Which for himself he offered, and
    the people's errors too:
  by which the Holy Ghost set forth
    a figure of the true:

4 That whilst the tabernacle stood,
    thereby it was expressed,
  The way into the Holiest
    was not made manifest:

5 A figure for that present time
    while divers vows were paid,
  with gifts and sacrifices burnt
    which oftentimes were made,

6 But could the off'rer not perfect,
    nor make the conscience clean,
  which stood in meats, drinks, washings that
    had oft and diverse been,

7 And also carnal ord'nances,
    which on them were imposed,
  until the reformation which
    the former ages closed.

Hymn 139

Hebrews 9:11-12

Orlington

1 CHRIST being come a great high priest
    of good things that shall be,
  by that more great and perfect place
    wherein abide doth he;

2 Not made with hands, that is to say,
    not of this building wrought;
  and neither by the blood of goats
    and calves which oft were brought:

3 But once into the holy place
    by his own blood went he,
  redemption having wrought for us
    which shall eternal be.

Hymn 140

Hebrews 9:19-23

London New

1 WHEN Moses in the law had read
   each precept from the book,
 unto the people all, the blood
   of calves and goats he took;

2 He also water, scarlet wool,
   and hyssop fresh did take,
 and sprinkled both the book and all
   the people, as he spake:

3 The blood, this, of the testament
   which God to you did give,
 and which to you he hath enjoined,
   that ye thereby might live.

4 The tabernacle with the blood
   moreover sprinkled he,
 and all the vessels that pertain
   unto the ministry.

5 And almost all things by the law
   are purged with blood alone;
 and save that blood is shed there can
   be no remission known.

6 'Twas therefore necessary that
   the patterns that applied
 to things high in the heavenlies
   with these be purified:

7 But that the very things themselves
    which in the heavens are
be purged with sacrifices which
    than these are better far.

Hymn 141
Hebrews 9:24-28
Wiltshire

1 FOR Christ himself is entered not,
    as those priests hitherto,
the holy places made with hands,
    the figures of the true,

2 But into heaven high itself
    that there he might abide
and in God's presence now appear
    for us for whom he died:

3 Nor yet himself to offer oft,
    as the high priest each year
did enter in the holy place
    and others' blood bring near:

4 For, since the world's foundation, oft
    must he have suffered then;
but now he in the world's end once
    appeared hath unto men,

5 That so he sin out of the way
    once and for all might take,
and be himself that sacrifice
    which doth atonement make.

6 And as men once must die, thenceforth
    in judgment to appear:

so Christ was offered once, the sins
   of many men to bear;
7 And unto them that look for him
   the second time shall he
appear without sin, unto all
   that by him saved shall be.

Hymn 142

Hebrews 10:1-4

S. Agnes

1 FOR of good things to come the law
      a shadow having proved
   and not the very image true
      of things far off removed,

2 Can ne'er with sacrifices which
      they offered year by year
   continually, the comers hence
      make perfect to appear.

3 For then would not the off'rings cease?
      because once purged and clean
   the worshippers no more of sins
      had vexed in conscience been.

4 But in those sacrifices slain
      each year ariseth doubt,
   because there is remembrance new
      of sins not blotted out.

5 For 'tis not possible that blood
      of bulls and goats shed then
   should ever purge or take away
      the sinfulness of men.

Hymn 143

Hebrews 10:5-9

Repton

1 WHEN he into the world doth come,
   No sacrifice, saith he,
 or off'ring would'st thou; for thou hast
   a body framed for me:

2 In off'rings that are burned with fire,
   and sacrificed for sin,
 no pleasure hadst thou, neither would'st
   thou take delight therein.

3 Then said I, Lo, I come, (of me
   'tis written hitherto
 within the volume of the book,)
   O God, thy will to do.

4 Above when said he, Sacrifice
   and off'ring under law,
 burnt off'rings too, and those for sin,
   thou would'st accept no more,

5 And neither pleasure hadst therein
   that oft-times offered be;
 then, Lo, I come to do thy will,
   O thou my God, saith he.

6 Those off'rings at the first required
   he therefore takes away,
 that he the second in their place
   establish ever may.

Hymn 144

Hebrews 10:10-13

Tiverton

1 ONCE and for ever sanctified
　　by his own will are we,
through Jesus Christ's slain body which
　　an off'ring make did he.

2 For every priest stands minist'ring
　　and off'ring up each day
the selfsame sacrifices, which
　　can ne'er take sins away:

3 But this man, when one sacrifice
　　he offered, and did die
for sins for ever, then sat down
　　at God's right hand on high;

4 That he from henceforth should abide
　　in sure expectancy,
till all his foes and enemies
　　his footstool made shall be.

Hymn 145

Hebrews 10:19-23

Salzburg

1 AS having therefore boldness which
　　faith doth to us afford,
to come into the holiest
　　by Jesus' precious blood,

2 By that which he hath made for us,
  a new and living way,
 as consecrated through the veil,
  his flesh, that is to say,

3 And with an high priest o'er God's house,
  let us to him draw near
 in full assurance of belief,
  true-hearted and sincere,

4 From an ill conscience having hearts
  that sprinkled now have been,
 and having also bodies that
  are washed with water clean:

5 Let us not waver, but hold fast
  our faith's profession sure,
 for he that gave the promise doth
  in faithfulness endure.

Hymn 146

Hebrews 10:28-30

Dundee

1 THE man that Moses' law despised
  did without mercy die,
 when two or three did witness bear
  and 'gainst him testify:

2 Of how much sorer punishment
  shall he be worthy thought,
 think ye, who hath the Son of God
  beneath his foot's tread brought,

3 And counted hath the cov'nant blood,
    which had him sanctified,
a thing unholy, and of grace
    the Spirit hath denied?

4 For him we know that said, Belongs
    the vengeance unto me:
I, saith the Lord, will recompense.
    The Lord the Judge shall be.

Hymn 147
Hebrews 10:35-39

Stracathro

1 NOW therefore cast ye not away
    your steadfast confidence,
which hath hereafter great reward
    and weighty recompense.

2 For ye have need of patience, that,
    when ye the will of God
have fully done, the promise he
    might unto you afford.

3 For yet a little while shall pass,
    and then assuredly,
behold, he that shall come, will come,
    and tarry not will he.

4 Now, as the scripture doth record,
    the just by faith shall live:
if one draw back, then to my soul
    he shall no pleasure give.

5 But we are not of them who back
  unto perdition draw,
 but of them that to save the soul
  believingly endure.

Hymn 148

Hebrews 11:3-7

Kingsfold

1 THROUGH faith perceive we that the worlds
   by God's word framed have been,
  that made from things which do appear
   was nothing that is seen.

2 By faith a sacrifice to God
   more excellent than Cain
  did Abel offer, by the which
   he witness did obtain,

3 God testifying of his gifts
   that he was justified;
  and by it still, though he were dead,
   yet doth his speech abide.

4 By faith translated Enoch was
   that death he should not see;
  and, since God had translated him,
   not found at all was he:

5 For he, ere he translated was,
   this testimony gave,
  that he pleased God: but without faith
   no pleasure can he have;

6 For he believe must that he is
    that cometh unto God;
  and that those who with diligence
    him seek he will reward.

7 By faith once Noah, warned of God
    of what did not appear,
  prepared an ark to save his house,
    as being moved with fear;

8 By which he did condemn the world,
    and was from henceforth known
  as heir of that same righteousness
    which is by faith alone.

Hymn 149

Hebrews 11:8-12

Crediton

1 BY faith aforetime Abraham,
    to go forth being made
  into a place which after he
    inherit should, obeyed;

2 By faith he went he knew not where,
    his dwelling oft to change,
  and sojourned in the promised land,
    as in a country strange;

3 In tabernacles he did dwell,
    though made of promise heir,
  with Isaac and with Jacob, who
    his heritage did share:

4 Because he for a city looked
   which hath foundations sure,
  which built hath been and made of God
   for ever to endure.

5 Through faith strength to conceive a child
   past age did Sarah have,
  because she judged him faithful that
   to her the promise gave.

6 And therefore sprang there e'en of one,
   and him as good as dead,
  a multitude like to the stars
   throughout the heavens spread:

7 And also like unto the sand,
   which found is by the sea,
  upon the shore innumerable,
   which cannot reckoned be.

Hymn 150

Hebrews 11:13-16

Covenanters

1 NOW these all died in faith: not one
   the promises received;
  but, seeing them afar, were all
   persuaded, and believed;

2 And did embrace them, and confessed
   that they were strangers all,
  yea, pilgrims passing through the earth,
   and sojourners withal.

3 For they that do a country seek
    thereby such things proclaim:
  and truly, had they mindful been
    of that land whence they came,

4 They might occasion then have had
    whereby they might return;
  but for a better country far,
    and heavenly, they yearn:

5 And therefore God is not ashamed
    called as their God to be,
  because a city yet to come
    prepared for them hath he.

Hymn 151

Hebrews 11:17-22

Psalm 107

1 BY faith, when Abraham was tried,
    he offered up his son:
  and he that had the promises,
    his sole begotten one,

2 Of whom it had before been said,
    when speak with him did he,
  That called in Isaac, thine own son,
    thy promised seed shall be:

3 For that God could, e'en from the dead,
    him raise up, he believed;
  from whence he in a figure him
    to life again received.

HEBREWS

4 By faith did Isaac call his sons,
   when by old age o'ercome,
  and Jacob he with Esau blessed
   concerning things to come.

5 By faith, when Jacob dying was,
   both Joseph's sons he blessed,
  and leaning on his staff, himself
   a worshipper confessed.

6 By faith when Joseph died, he first
   of Isr'el's leaving spake;
  and, as concerning his own bones,
   did strict commandment make.

Hymn 152

Hebrews 11:23-29

S. Mirren

1 BY faith did Moses' parents cause
     him hid three months to be;
  nor feared the king, because they saw
   a proper child was he.

2 By faith when Moses came to years,
   the honour he did shun
  of being favoured with the name
   of Pharaoh's daughter's son;

3 He rather with God's people chose
   to bear affliction's pain,
  than for a season to enjoy
   sin's passing pleasures vain;

4 Esteeming Christ's reproach more rich
    than Egypt's treasure-hoard:
  for he had to the recompense
    respect of the reward.

5 By faith he Egypt's land forsook,
    nor did the king's wrath fear:
  endured he, as him seeing who
    doth not to sight appear.

6 Through faith he kept the passover
    and sprinkling of the blood,
  lest he the first-born that destroyed
    should hurt to them afford.

7 By faith they through the Red sea passed
    as on the dry land found,
  which the Egyptians when they did
    assay to do were drowned.

Hymn 153

Hebrews 11:30-34

Brother James' Air

1 BY faith the walls of Jericho
    fell at the people's shout,
  when them they after seven days
    had compassed round about.

2 By faith the harlot Rahab, when
    she had with peace received

the spies from Isr'el, perished not
   with them that disbelieved.

3 And what shall I more say? for time
      would fail to tell at length
   of Gideon, of Barak, and
      of Samson in his strength,

4 Of Jephthah, and of David, yea,
      and chosen Samuel too,
   and of the prophets: who through faith
      whole kingdoms did subdue;

5 They righteousness did work, and did
      the promises obtain;
   they stopped the mouths of rav'ning lions,
      and safe were found again;

6 The vi'lence of the fire they quenched,
      escaped the sword's edge quite;
   they out of weakness were made strong,
      waxed valiant in the fight.

Hymn 154

Hebrews 11:34-40

Wondrous Love
(refrain slightly adapted)

1 THE armies of the aliens
      to flight by faith they turned;
   their womenfolk their dead received
      again to life returned;

2 And others tortured were, and would
    accept of no reprieve;
  a better resurrection that
    they might at last receive;

3 And others trial of mockings had,
    and scourgings cruel and sore;
  of bonds and of imprisonment,
    which long they did endure:

4 They stoned were, they were sawn in half,
    they tempted were in vain,
  they in the hatred of their foes
    were with the sword's edge slain:

5 In sheepskins and in goatskins clad
    they wandered destitute,
  whilst their tormentors did them oft
    afflict and persecute;

6 (Of whom the world unworthy was:)
    in deserts wandered they,
  in mountains, dens, caves of the earth,
    in peril night and day.

7 And these, as having all obtained
    through faith a good report,
  did in their lifetime not receive
    the promise which they sought:

8 God having a provision made
    whereby obtain might we
  some better thing: that without us
    they should not perfect be.

Hymn 155

Hebrews 12:3-8

Spohr

1. CONSIDER him who patiently
    did 'gainst himself endure
   from sinful and unholy men
    such contradiction sore:

2. Lest ye be wearied in your minds,
    and faint your hearts within:
   to blood ye have resisted not
    in striving against sin.

3. And ye the exhortation have
    forgotten, which doth speak
   to you as unto children found
    of disposition meek:

4. Despise not, thou that art my son,
    the chast'ning of the Lord,
   nor faint when unto thee he doth
    a just rebuke reward:

5. For whom he loves the Lord doth make
    by chast'ning sore to grieve,
   and scourgeth every son whom he
    doth to himself receive.

6. God dealeth with you as with sons
    if chast'ning ye endure;
   for what son is he that escapes
    the father's chast'ning sore?

HYMNS OF THE NEW TESTAMENT

7 If ye are spared the rod, whereof
     all must partakers be,
   then manifestly bastards ill
     and not his sons are ye.

HYMN 156
Hebrews 12:14-17

Gerontius

1 WITH all men follow after peace,
     and seek with one accord
   for holiness: that without which
     no man shall see the Lord.

2 Look diligently lest at last
     one of God's grace should fail;
   lest any root of bitterness
     should springing up prevail,

3 And thereby many be defiled;
     lest any there should be
   that fornicate, or anyone
     marked by profanity;

4 As Esau, who his birthright sold
     for but one scrap of meat:
   yet afterwards he to possess
     the blessing did entreat;

5 But was rejected: for no place
     find to repent did he,
   although he afterwards with tears
     sought for it carefully.

Hymn 157

Hebrews 12:18-25

Stroudwater

1 NOT to the mount that might be touched,
     with fire encompassed round,
 nor blackness, darkness, tempest great,
     nor to the trumpet's sound,

2 Nor to the voice of words come ye:
     which voice they prayed who heard
 that henceforth spoken unto them
     no more should be the word:

3 (For that which was commanded them
     no more endure could they:
 And if a beast but touch the mount,
     it should be stoned straightway,

4 Or else a dart should thrust it through.
     So dreadful was the sight
 that Moses did declare, I quake
     exceedingly with fright:)

5 But ye are to mount Sion come
     that doth in height excel,
 and to the city in the which
     the living God doth dwell:

6 And come unto Jerusalem
     the heavenly are ye,
 and angels that in company
     innumerable be,

HYMNS OF THE NEW TESTAMENT

7 To the assembly general,
   and first-born church withal,
 which written are in heaven, and
   to God the Judge of all,

8 And to the spirits of just men
   brought to a perfect state,
 to Jesus, who the cov'nant new
   on high doth mediate,

9 And to the sprinkling of the blood,
   that better things doth speak
 than that of Abel, from the ground
   which doth for vengeance seek.

10 Now unto him that speaks see that
    ye no refusal make.
 If they escaped not who refused
    him on the earth that spake,

11 Much more then shall not we escape,
    if we should turn away
 from him that doth from heaven speak,
    his word to disobey.

Hymn 158

Hebrews 13:11-14

S. Mary

1 THE bodies of those beasts, whose blood
       within the sanctuary
  the high priest brought for sin, without
       the camp consumed must be.

2 Whence Jesus also, that he might
   the people sanctify
with his own blood, in suffering
   without the gate did die.

3 Let us go therefore unto him,
   and to that place repair
that is without the camp, so that
   we his reproach might bear.

4 Because no city here that is
   continuing have we,
but seek we one to come that shall
   for ever stablished be.

Hymn 159

Hebrews 13:20-21

Torwood

1 THE God of peace, that did again
   out of death's darkness deep
bring our Lord Jesus, even that
   great shepherd of the sheep,

2 Through the eternal cov'nant blood,
   you perfect make to be,
in every work of good, his will
   to do with constancy,

3 As working in you that which is
   well pleasing him before,
through Jesus Christ, to whom belongs
   the glory evermore.

HYMN 160

James 1:2-6   *S. Stephen*

1 WHEN ye into temptations great
    and manifold do fall,
  rejoice, my brethren, and be glad,
    and joyous count it all.

2 This knowing, that your trial of faith,
    if suffered patiently,
  works patience perfect and entire,
    that nothing wanting be.

3 If one lack wisdom, let him ask
    of God that unto all
  gives lib'rally, upbraiding not:
    and give to him he shall.

4 But let him ask in faith, and not
    as wavering; for he
  that wavereth is like a wave
    wind-tossed upon the sea.

HYMN 161

James 1:16-21   *Richmond*

1 DO not, my brethren well beloved,
    to error give assent.
  For every good and perfect gift
    from high above is sent,

2 Descending from the Father true
    of lights, with whom is found

no variation, neither shade
cast by a turning round.

3 Beget us with the word of truth
of his own will did he,
that we a kind of first-fruits should
e'en of his creatures be.

4 Wherefore, my brethren well beloved,
let every man of you
be swift to hearken, slow to speak,
and slow wrath to pursue:

5 Because the wrath of man works not
the righteousness of God.
Now therefore do ye lay aside
all filthiness abhorred,

6 And put all superfluity
of naughtiness apart,
receiving the engrafted word
with meekness in your heart.

Hymn 162
James 1:26-27

S. Fulbert

1 IF there among you any man
religious seem to be,
and bridleth not his tongue, deceived
in his own heart is he:

2 This man's religion's vain. But that
found undefiled and pure
in God and in the Father's sight
doth on this wise endure:

3 To visit oft the fatherless,
 and widows vexed that weep,
 and that a man should from the world
 himself unspotted keep.

Hymn 163
James 2:8-13

Bristol

1 IF ye fulfil the royal law
 of which the scriptures tell,
 Thy neighbour love e'en as thyself,
 ye do exceeding well:

2 But if ye persons should respect,
 then sin do ye commit,
 and as transgressors of the law
 convinced are every whit.

3 For whoso shall the whole law keep,
 and yet in one point fall,
 he hath offended 'gainst the whole,
 and guilty is of all.

4 For he that said, Do not commit
 adultery, said too,
 Kill not. Now if thou break the one,
 but dost the other do,

5 The law itself thou hast transgressed.
 So speak, and so do ye,
 as those that shall be judged e'en by
 the law of liberty.

6 For judgment merciless he'll have
   that did no mercy show.
   'Gainst judgment mercy doth rejoice
   her favour to bestow.

Hymn 164

James 2:14-20

S. Flavian

1 WHAT profit, brethren, doth appear,
   though one should faith confess
  and have not works? Can faith him save
   who doth but words profess?

2 Should there a brother be unclothed,
   or sister naked found,
  and destitute of daily food,
   or with affliction bound,

3 And one of you say unto them,
   Depart ye now in peace,
  and be ye warmed and filled, and may
   your comfort much increase:

4 Yet notwithstanding ye give not
   the things for which they plead,
  what profit are thy words to them
   to meet their present need?

5 Behold, 'tis even so with faith
   in which but words are shown;
  for it, if destitute of works,
   is dead and found alone.

HYMNS OF THE NEW TESTAMENT

6 Yea, Thou hast faith, and I have works,
    a man may testify;
  show me thy faith without thy works:
    mine show by works will I.

7 One God thou dost believe: 'tis well.
    The devils this believe;
  they also tremble: what effect
    in thee can we perceive?

8 But wilt thou know and understand,
    O vain and empty man,
  that faith found without works is dead,
    and nothing profit can?

Hymn 165

James 3:8-12

Hebdomadal

1 NO man the tongue can tame: it is
    an evil none can rule;
  yea, 'tis a member that is found
    of deadly poison full.

2 Therewith God, e'en the Father, we
    do bless with gratitude;
  and therewith curse we men, made in
    God's own similitude.

3 Out of one mouth there doth proceed
    a blessing and a curse:
  such things, my brethren, should not be,
    which make our speech perverse.

JAMES

4 Doth at one place a fountain-head
    send water that is sweet
and bitter also? can the fig
    bear olives one can eat?

5 Or can the vine bear figs? Just so
    a fountain can no more
at once with water that is salt
    fresh water also pour.

Hymn 166
James 4:13-17

Redhead No. 66

1 GO to now, ye that say, Today,
    or soon, we go again
to such a city for a year,
    to buy and sell for gain:

2 Whereas ye know not what shall be
    upon the morrow found.
What is your life? A vapour which
    appeareth o'er the ground;

3 And in a while it vanisheth.
    For that ye ought to say,
If that the Lord will, we shall live,
    and do such things this day.

4 But now ye in your boastings joy,
    though all such joy is ill:
he therefore sins that good doth know,
    but doth it not fulfil.

Hymn 167
James 5:16-20

Evan

1. TO one another own your faults,
    and for each other pray,
   that by this means ye might be healed,
    and no more go astray.

2. The fervent prayer effectual
    a righteous man doth make
   availeth much; Elias, now,
    for an example take:

3. Though subject to like passions strong,
    yet earnestly he prayed
   that rain might cease: three years, six months,
    rain from the earth was stayed.

4. At length he bowed to pray once more:
    then gave the heavens rain,
   and watered all the thirsty earth,
    which brought forth fruit again.

5. If, brethren, any of you err,
    far from the truth to go,
   and one thereafter him convert,
    let him most surely know,

6. That from the error of his way
    he that the sinner wins
   shall save a soul from death, and hide
    a multitude of sins.

Hymn 168
I Peter 1:1-2

Rest

1 FROM Peter, an apostle sent,
  whom Jesus Christ did call,
unto the strangers scattered far
  throughout the regions all,

2 Of God the Father the elect
  whom first foreknow did he,
through holiness the Spirit wrought
  in you abundantly,

3 Unto the sure obedience
  and sprinkling of the blood
of Jesus Christ: Grace unto you,
  and peace, be multiplied.

Hymn 169
I Peter 1:3-8

Gräfenberg

1 OF our Lord Jesus Christ the God
  and Father blessed be,
for after his own mercy great
  begotten us hath he,

2 Unto a lively hope by that
  of which we testify,
the resurrection from the dead
  of Jesus Christ on high,

3 To an enduring heritage
  for evermore preserved,

unfading, undefiled, for you
　　in heaven high reserved,

4　Who to salvation, by God's power,
　　　are kept through faith always,
　which ready is to be revealed
　　　when come the latter days.

5　Wherein ye greatly joy, though now,
　　　awhile, if need there be,
　through sore temptations manifold,
　　　in heaviness are ye:

6　That of your faith the trial, which doth
　　　more precious far abide
　than finest gold which perisheth,
　　　though it with fire be tried,

7　Might found to praise and honour be,
　　　and glory from above,
　when Jesus Christ himself appears,
　　　whom, seeing not, ye love:

8　In whom, though now ye see him not,
　　　yet ye your faith employ,
　and do with joy unspeakable
　　　and full of glory joy.

Hymn 170

I Peter 1:13-17　　　　　　　*Stracathro*

1　GIRD up your minds, be vigilant,
　　　and hope unto the end
　for grace brought nigh when Jesus Christ
　　　from heaven shall descend;

I PETER

2 As children that with joy obey,
　　not fashioned or renewed
according to the former lusts
　　in ignorance pursued:

3 But as he which hath called you doth
　　in holiness abound,
so holy in all manner be
　　of conversation found:

4 For it is written, Holy be,
　　for holy I appear.
And if ye on the Father call,
　　the time pass ye in fear,

5 Whilst here ye sojourn: for without
　　respect to persons shown,
according unto each man's work,
　　made is his judgment known.

Hymn 171
I Peter 1:18-21　　　　　　　　　*S. Columba*

1 BELOVED brethren, know ye all
　　that not redeemed were ye
with silver and with gold, or things
　　corruptible that be;

2 From your vain conversation which
　　ye did of man receive
by that tradition which afore
　　your fathers did you leave;

3 But with the precious blood of Christ
　　which shed for you hath been,

as of a pure unblemished lamb,
　　that without spot is seen:

4 Who foreordained was ere that he
　　the world's foundation laid,
but in these latter times for you
　　hath manifest been made,

5 Who by him do believe in God,
　　raised up by his right hand
from death to glory; that your faith
　　and hope in God might stand.

Hymn 172
I Peter 1:22-25

S. Peter

1 SEE that ye one another love
　　with pure heart fervently:
for not of seed corruptible
　　been born again have ye,

2 But of seed incorruptible,
　　by that same word of God
which liveth and for evermore
　　doth have assured abode.

3 For all flesh is as grass, and all
　　man's glory as its flower;
the grass doth wither, and the same
　　doth perish in that hour:

4 But of the Lord the word endures
　　abiding ever new,
which by the gospel is the word
　　that preached is unto you.

Hymn 173
I Peter 2:1-5

Caroline

1 ALL malice laying to one side,
    with every form of guile,
hypocrisies, yea, envies, and
    all utterances vile,

2 As new-born babes, desire the milk
    which through the word doth flow,
at once sincere and nourishing,
    that ye thereby may grow:

3 If so be ye have tasted that
    most gracious is the Lord.
To whom approaching, to a stone
    which doth you life afford,

4 One disallowed indeed of men,
    whom they at will reject,
but one that chosen is of God,
    both precious and elect,

5 Ye also, choice and lively stones,
    which fitly framed have been,
are as a dwelling spiritual,
    an holy priesthood, seen;

6 That sacrifices spiritual
    now offer up may ye,
which unto God by Jesus Christ
    acceptable shall be.

HYMN 174
I Peter 2:6-10

Petersham

1 IN scripture 'tis contained, Behold,
    for lay do I alone
in Zion, precious and elect,
    a chief and corner stone:

2 And he that doth on him believe
    shall not confounded be.
Most precious therefore unto you
    which do believe is he:

3 But unto those gainsayers which
    have always disobeyed,
the stone the builders disallowed
    head corner-stone is made,

4 Besides a stumbling-stone, and rock
    of sore offence alway,
to them that stumble at the word,
    and do it disobey:

5 Whereunto also they were all
    appointed and decreed.
But ye of the election are,
    a truly chosen seed:

6 A royal priesthood ye are called,
    a nation sanctified,
a people most peculiar,
    set for himself aside;

7 That ye his praises should show forth,
    and in the same delight,

who hath you out of darkness called
   into his marv'llous light:
8 Once not a people, now are ye
   the people of God's choice:
once without mercy, now therein
   with gladness ye rejoice.

Hymn 175

I Peter 2:21-25   S. Mary

1 CHRIST suffered for us, and thereby
      did an example leave,
   that ye should follow in his steps
      that do on him believe:

2 Who did no sin, and neither once
      found in his mouth was guile:
   who, when he was of men reviled,
      did not again revile.

3 He, when he suffered, threatened not;
      but did himself commit
   to him that judgeth righteously,
      and to him did submit:

4 Who his own self did bear our sins
      by suff'ring in our stead
   in his own body on the tree;
      that we, to sins as dead,

5 Should by him unto righteousness
      our lives henceforward live,
   healed by his stripes who in our place
      himself did for us give.

6 For once ye strayed as sheep, but now
    returned to him are ye,
 the Shepherd and the Bishop who
    your souls doth oversee.

Hymn 176
I Peter 4:10-11

York

1 AS each man hath received the gift
    so minister the same,
 that ye might God's grace manifold
    as stewards good proclaim.

2 If any speak, as oracles
    of God let this be done;
 or minister, as with the power
    God gives to every one:

3 That God through Jesus Christ may be
    in all things glorified,
 to whom praise and dominion be,
    for ever to abide.

Hymn 177
I Peter 4:16-19

Lloyd

1 IF one should suffer ill because
    he as a Christian live,
 then let that man, as unashamed,
    to God the glory give.

I PETER

2 At God's house judgment must begin:
    if first at us, I say,
what shall the end be of them that
    God's gospel disobey?

3 And if the righteous scarce be saved,
    forewarned of him to fear,
where shall ungodly men and those
    that sinners are appear?

4 Wherefore let them that suffer grief,
    according to God's will,
commit their souls in doing well
    to their Creator still.

Hymn 178
I Peter 5:7-11

S. Kilda

1 UPON him cast ye all your care,
    for care for you doth he.
At all times with sobriety
    be vigilant do ye;

2 The devil, as a roaring lion,
    your adversary sore,
about you walketh, seeking out
    those whom he may devour:

3 Whom steadfast in the faith resist,
    for these same trials pertain
to your afflicted brethren which
    do in the world remain.

4 But now the God of every grace,
     who hath us called in love
  to his eternal glory by
     Christ Jesus from above,

5 When once ye suffered have awhile,
     you perfect make to be,
  and stablish, strengthen, settle you,
     in truth and verity.

6 Now unto him to whom alone
     the glory doth pertain,
  dominion be through ages all,
     for evermore. Amen.

Hymn 179
II Peter 1:1-4

S. Frances

1 FROM Simon Peter, servant, and
     apostle true ordained
  of Jesus Christ, to them that have
     like precious faith obtained,

2 With us through that same righteousness
     which is of God expressed,
  and of our Saviour Jesus Christ
     abroad made manifest:

3 May grace and peace be multiplied,
     and unto you assured,
  through that which may be known of God
     and Jesus our own Lord;

II PETER

4 According as his pow'r divine
   hath caused us to obtain
all things that do both unto life
   and godliness pertain,

5 E'en through the knowledge from above
   of him who did us call
unto the glory that is his,
   and virtue pure withal:

6 Whence great and precious promises
   give unto us did he,
whereby of that which is divine
   ye might partakers be.

Hymn 180
II Peter 1:5-10
Dunfermline

1 MY brethren, with all diligence
   to faith add virtue true;
to virtue knowledge; then do ye
   add temperance thereto;

2 To temperance next patience add;
   to patience join besides
all godliness; and kindness, too,
   that brotherly abides;

3 And love to kindness brotherly.
   If in you these abound,
enduring still, ye shall not once
   be dry or barren found;

4 For they you make that without fruit
   ye shall no more remain,

in what to our Lord Jesus Christ
   in knowledge doth pertain.

5 But he that lacks these things is blind,
     and cannot far off see,
   and hath forgotten that once purged
     from his old sins was he.

6 Wherefore the rather diligence
     give ye unto your call
   to make your own election sure,
     that ye may never fall.

Hymn 181
II Peter 1:15-21

S. Anne

1 I WILL endeavour to the last
     that ye may able be
   on my decease to keep these things
     always in memory.

2 We cunning fables followed not
     when we to you expressed
   of our Lord Jesus Christ the power
     and coming manifest;

3 For we his majesty beheld
     what time that honour due
   and glory also he received
     from God the Father true.

4 For came there such a voice to him,
     from glory far on high:
   This is mine own beloved Son,
     in whom well pleased am I.

II PETER

5 This is the voice that we did hear,
   which did from heaven sound,
 when with him in the holy mount
   together we were found.

6 We also have of prophecy
   a more sure word indeed,
 whereunto ye yourselves do well
   that ye take earnest heed,

7 As to a light that shines within
   a place where darkness lies,
 till day dawn, and the day-star bright
   shall in your hearts arise;

8 This knowing first: no prophecy
   that scripture doth contain
 is such that an interpreter
   can privately explain:

9 For prophecy came not of old
   by that in which men boast,
 but holy men of God spake forth,
   moved by the Holy Ghost.

Hymn 182
II Peter 2:1-3

Dundee

1 AS 'mong the people of old time
   there were false prophets found,
 so also even in your midst
   false teachers shall abound,

193

2 Who heresies most damnable
    shall bring in privily,
so that the Lord that purchased them
    they even should deny,

3 And on themselves bring judgment swift:
    yet many follow shall
their grievous ways, and cause reproach
    upon truth's way to fall.

4 For they through covetousness ill
    shall crafty schemes devise,
that they might with feigned words thereby
    of you make merchandise:

5 Whose judgment of a long time since
    doth linger now no more,
and their damnation, slumb'ring not,
    nigh unto them doth draw.

Hymn 183
II Peter 3:2-7

Culross

1 MIND ye the holy prophets' words,
        with that commandment new
   the Lord and Saviour gave by us
        his own apostles true.

2 This knowing first, that there shall come
        those that with scoffing talk,
   which in the last days wantonly
        in their own lusts shall walk:

II PETER

3 Where is his promised coming now?
    is that which they shall say,
For since the fathers fell asleep
    all things unaltered stay.

4 For they through willingness of this
    with ignorance are bold,
that even by the word of God
    the heavens were of old;

5 Out of the water stood the earth,
    and in the water too:
whereby the world that was of old
    the deluge overthrew:

6 But both the heavens and the earth
    which at this time exist,
by that same word are kept in store
    and suffered to subsist,

7 Reserved unto the coming fire
    against that great day when
both judgment and perdition swift
    shall fall on godless men.

Hymn 184

II Peter 3:8-14

Old 18th

1 BELOVED, be not ignorant
      that to the Lord appears
a thousand years as but one day,
    one day a thousand years.

HYMNS OF THE NEW TESTAMENT

2 For verily none slackness can
    put to the Lord's account
  concerning his own promise true,
    as some men slackness count;

3 But he long-suff'ring is to us,
    not willing e'en that one
  should ever perish, but that all
    should to repentance come.

4 For as a thief comes in the night
    so comes the Lord's great day,
  in which with an exceeding noise
    the heavens pass away;

5 The elements themselves shall melt
    with heat of great degree,
  the earth and all the works therein
    burned up with fire shall be.

6 Since all these things shall be dissolved,
    what kind of persons sound
  ought ye to be in holiness
    and godly conduct found:

7 Both looking for, and hasting to,
    the day of God to come,
  wherein the heavens, all aflame,
    shall quite dissolved become;

8 And wherein all the elements
    and substances entire
  shall likewise melt with fervent heat
    and pass away in fire?

9 But by his promise look we for
      new heavens nonetheless,
   and for a new-created earth,
      wherein dwells righteousness.

10 Since for such things ye look, belov'd,
      give diligence that ye
   found spotless, yea, and without blame,
      of him in peace may be.

Hymn 185
I John 1:1-3

French

1 THAT which from the beginning was,
      which heard we verily,
   which we with our own eyes have seen,
      which looked upon have we,

2 Which handled have our hands, of that
      true Word of life unseen;
   (for manifested was the life,
      and we the same have seen,

3 And witness bear, and show to you
      that life eternal bless'd,
   which with the Father dwelt, and was
      to us made manifest;)

4 That which we have both seen and heard
      we unto you declare,
   that thereby also ye with us
      in fellowship may share.

5 And verily our fellowship
    is with the Father one,
in unity with Jesus Christ,
    his sole begotten Son.

Hymn 186

I John 1:4-10

Elgin

1 AND these things unto you we write,
       that full your joy may be.
   This then in truth the message is
       which heard of him have we:

2 That God is light; and that in him
       no darkness doth reside.
   If we do say that we with him
       in fellowship abide,

3 And yet in darkness walk, we lie,
       and not the truth do we.
   But if we in the light do walk,
       as in the light is he,

4 We fellowship together have
       as we do walk therein;
   and his Son Jesus Christ's own blood
       doth cleanse us from all sin.

5 If we say that we have no sin,
       we do ourselves deceive,
   and in us truth is not, nor yet
       do we the same receive.

I JOHN

6 Because he faithful is and just,
     if we our sins confess,
  us to forgive our sins, and cleanse
     from all unrighteousness.

7 If we should say we have not sinned,
     then altogether we
  a liar make him, and his word
     within us cannot be.

Hymn 187
I John 2:1-6 *Kilmarnock*

1 MY little children, that no more
       ye sin, these things write I.
   Yet if one sin, there is for us
       an advocate on high;

2 'Tis Jesus Christ, the righteous one,
       unto the Father near:
   and the propitiation he
       doth for our sins appear;

3 Moreover not for ours alone,
       but also he abides
   the one propitiatory
       for all the world besides.

4 And hereby also we do know
       that him we know indeed,
   if his commandments all we keep,
       and to the same give heed.

5 He that doth say that him he knows,
       yet his commands keeps not,

a liar is, without the truth,
which in him be cannot.

6 But whoso keeps his word, in him
    shall God's love verily
perfected be: hereby we know
    that found in him are we.

7 He that saith he abides in him,
    professing him to know,
himself ought also so to walk
    as he did walk below.

Hymn 188
I John 2:7-11 *London New*

1 I, BRETHREN, write no new command,
    as hereby ye perceive,
but that commandment old which ye
    did from the first receive.

2 The old commandment is the word
    which from the first ye heard.
Again a new commandment I
    write to you through this word:

3 Which thing is alway true in him,
    and also now in you:
for past the dark is, and the light
    now shineth that is true.

4 He that saith he is in the light,
    and doth his brother hate,
doth even now until this hour
    abide in darkness great.

I JOHN

5 But he that doth his brother love
    abideth in the light,
and in him none occasion is
    whereby he stumble might.

6 He blind is that his brother hates,
    his walk in darkness lies;
he knows not where he goes, because
    that darkness blinds his eyes.

Hymn 189
I John 2:12-17
Jackson

1 NOW therefore unto you I write,
    my little children true,
because for his name's sake your sins
    have been forgiven you.

2 And unto you that fathers are
    moreover write I this,
because that ye have known him that
    from the beginning is.

3 And unto you I write, young men,
    that overcomers be,
because it is the wicked one
    that overcome have ye.

4 I, infants, write to you to whom
    the Father hath been shown.
I, fathers, wrote to you, for him
    ye from the first have known.

5 And unto you I wrote, young men,
    for strong have ye become,
  and in you dwells God's word, and ye
    the Wicked have o'ercome.

6 Love not the world, nor yet the things
    that in the world abound.
  Who loves the world, the Father's love
    within him is not found.

7 All in the world, its lust of flesh
    and eyes, withal life's pride,
  is of the Father not, but e'en
    doth of the world abide.

8 The world doth pass away; its lust
    doth likewise not endure:
  but he that do'th the will of God
    abideth evermore.

Hymn 190

I John 2:18-22

Wigtown

1 NOW, infants, it the last time is:
    and as declare did we
  to you that antichrist should come,
    so now come forth is he:

2 For there are many antichrists
    already gone abroad;
  whereby that it the last time is
    we know and are assured.

3 They went out from us, but they were
    not of us; had they been,

they would have stayed; but went, that they
    not of us might be seen.

4 But ye yourselves an unction have
    sent forth assuredly
from him that is the Holy One,
    and know all things do ye.

5 I wrote not unto you because
    the truth ye do not heed;
for it ye know, and that no lie
    doth from the truth proceed.

6 Who is a liar, but he that
    doth by his speech deny
that Jesus is the very Christ,
    as truth doth testify?

Hymn 191

I John 2:22-29

Gloucester

1 HE antichrist is, that denies
    the Father and the Son.
Whoso denies the Son, the same
    hath not the Father known.

2 Let therefore that in you abide
    which ye at first did hear:
if that within you shall remain
    to which ye first gave ear,

3 Continue in the Son and in
    the Father then shall ye.
His promise is eternal life,
    which promised us hath he.

4 These things to you I written have
 concerning those each one
that do seduce you, that afar
 out of the way have gone.

5 But the anointing, which of him
 received in truth have ye,
in you abides, and ye need not
 that one your teacher be:

6 But as the same doth all things teach,
 and truth is, and no lie,
e'en as it hath you taught, ye shall
 abide in him thereby.

7 Now, little children, dwell in him:
 that, when appear shall he,
before his coming unashamed
 have confidence may we.

8 If that he righteous is ye know,
 the knowledge ye possess
that every one is born of him
 that doeth righteousness.

Hymn 192
I John 3:7-11

1 MY little children, let none you *Rest*
 deceive with subtlety:
for he that doeth righteousness
 is righteous, as is he.

2 He of the devil is that doth
 commit and practise sin;

I JOHN

   because the devil sinned hath since
      the world did first begin.
3 God's Son was manifested that
      this cause fulfil might he,
   that of the devil all the works
      by him destroyed might be.
4 Whatever man is born of God
      commits not sin again,
   because within that man his seed
      doth constantly remain:
5 Nor can he sin, as born of God.
      Thus manifest indeed
   those children are that be of God,
      and those, the devil's seed:
6 Whoso doth not do righteousness
      is not from God above,
   and neither also is he that
      doth not his brother love.
7 Because that this the message is
      which from the first heard ye,
   that one another at all times
      love fervently should we.

Hymn 193
I John 4:4-6
Kilsyth

1 YE, little children, are of God,
      and overcome them do:
   for greater than he in the world
      is he that is in you.

HYMNS OF THE NEW TESTAMENT

2 For they, whom ye have overcome,
   do of the world appear;
 and therefore speak they of the world,
   and them the world doth hear.

3 We are of God: he heareth us
   that knowledge hath of God;
 he that is not of God doth not
   give ear unto our word.

4 Hereby the Spirit we do know
   that is of verity;
 and likewise know the spirit that
   of error is do we.

Hymn 194

I John 4:7-13

Morven

1 LOVE each the other one, for love
      doth God on us bestow;
 each one that loves is born of God,
   and thereby God doth know.

2 For he that loves not knows not God,
   because that God is love.
 Thus manifested was to us
   the love of God above:

3 Because that God into the world
   his sole begotten Son
 sent forth from heaven high that we
   might live through him alone.

4 For love is not that we loved God,
   but that love us did he,

and sent his Son who for our sins
  should an appeasement be:

5 Belov'd, if God hath so loved us
  from heaven far above,
we also ought to follow him,
  and one another love.

6 None hath seen God at any time.
  If love his own do we,
God in us dwells: and in us shall
  his love perfected be.

7 Hereby we know we in him dwell,
  and he in us doth live,
because he freely unto us
  doth of his Spirit give.

Hymn 195
I John 4:14-16

Invocation

1 AND we have seen, and unto you
  our witness do make known,
That as the Saviour of the world
  the Father sent the Son.

2 Whoso of Jesus shall confess
  that he is Son of God,
God in him dwelleth, and he shall
  in God have his abode.

3 And we have known and have believed
  the love of God above
which manifested was to us,
  for God himself is love:

4 And whosoever dwells in love,
   in God withal resides;
moreover it is true of God
   that he in him abides.

Hymn 196

I John 4:17-21

S. Kilda

1 HEREIN our love is perfect made,
      that boldness have may we
in judgment's day: for as he is,
   so in this world we be.

2 Love hath no fear, but perfect love
      makes not to be afraid;
fear torment hath: who feareth is
   in love not perfect made.

3 We love him, for he first loved us.
      If one should testify,
God love I, but his brother hate,
   behold, that man doth lie:

4 For he that loves his brother not,
      whom he hath plainly seen,
how can he then love God, the one
   that is by him unseen?

5 Moreover this commandment we
      do have from him above,
That he who loveth God should then
   his brother also love.

Hymn 197

I John 5:5-13 *Ellacombe*

1. WHO is he that shall of the world
    an overcomer be,
  but he of Jesus that believes
    that Son of God is he?

2. 'Tis he, e'en Jesus Christ, that came
    by water and by blood;
  nor yet by water only, but
    by water and by blood.

3. And witness doth the Spirit bear:
    for truth itself is he.
  And three there are that record bear,
    whose witness doth agree:

4. The Spirit, water, and the blood;
    these three are to one point:
  their testimony is but one,
    their witness is conjoint.

5. If we men's witness do receive,
    God's greater doth abide:
  this is the witness of his Son
    which God hath testified.

6. He that believeth on God's Son
    the witness hath received:
  but he hath God a liar made
    who hath not him believed;

7. For he the record hath denied
    that God gave of his Son.

This is the record: God us gave
  eternal life each one.

8 This life is in his Son: who hath
    the Son hath life indeed:
  without God's Son none hath the life
    that doth from him proceed.

9 These things I written have to you
    that on the name believe
  of him that is the Son of God,
    the witness to receive:

10 That thereby ye may know that ye
    eternal life possess,
  and of God's Son that ye the name
    believe may and confess.

HYMN 198
I John 5:18-21

Crimond

1 THAT whosoe'er is born of God
    doth sin not, know do we;
  and him the Wicked toucheth not,
    for keep himself doth he.

2 And know we that we are of God,
    and all the world besides
  held captive by the wicked one
    in wickedness abides.

3 And know we that God's Son is come,
    upon us to bestow
  an understanding from above,
    him that is true to know;

II JOHN

4 And in him that is true are we,
   e'en Jesus Christ his Son.
   True God is he, who hath to us
   eternal life made known.

5 My little children, take ye heed,
   and be ye ware of men;
   and likewise do ye keep yourselves
   from idols all. Amen.

Hymn 199

II John 6-11

Old 22nd

1 THAT we should one another love,
   heard from the first have we,
   and after his commandments walk,
   for this is charity.

2 And this is the commandment, That
   as ye from us have heard
   and learned from the beginning, ye
   should walk in this same word.

3 Deceivers many entering
   into the world there be,
   of Jesus Christ who say not that
   come in the flesh is he.

4 They liars are, and antichrist,
   that to deceive have sought.
   Look to yourselves, that we lose not
   those things which we have wrought;

5 But that we gain a full reward.
  For whoso doth transgress,
and in Christ's doctrine not abide,
  he doth not God possess.

6 He in the doctrine that abides
    that is of Christ made known,
he verily possesseth both
    the Father and the Son.

7 If one there come to you without
    this doctrine, take ye heed:
receive him not into your house,
    nor bid ye him Godspeed;

8 For he that biddeth him Godspeed
    thereby the truth forsakes,
and of the evil of his deeds
    and errors he partakes.

Hymn 200
III John 2-8

Sawley

1 BELOV'D, I wish above all things
    that thou may'st prosp'rous be,
and kept in health, e'en as thy soul
    enjoys prosperity.

2 I much rejoiced when brethren came
    and of thee testified,
that, as thou walkest in the truth,
    truth in thee doth abide.

III JOHN

3 I have no greater joy than this,
    to hear the brethren say
that those which are my children dear
    walk in the truth alway.

4 Belov'd, thou doest faithfully
    whatever thou dost do
to brethren and to strangers, which
    of thee bear witness true;

5 For of thy love they tell the church:
    whom if thou forward bring
upon their way in godliness,
    thou do'st a goodly thing:

6 Because that in their going forth
    they went for his name's sake,
and nothing did they in the way
    from any Gentile take.

7 Such therefore ought we to receive,
    that fellow helpers we
together with them to the truth
    might thereby prove to be.

HYMN 201
III John 11-12, 14

Duke's Tune

1 BELOV'D, ill follow not, but good.
       Because of God is he
that doeth good: but see not God
    shall those that evil be.

2 All speak well of Demetrius,
 so doth the truth besides;
yea, we bear record, and ye know
 our record true abides.

3 I trust to see thee face to face:
 I peace to thee proclaim.
Our friends thee salutation give:
 greet thou the friends by name.

HYMN 202

Jude 1-3

Caithness

1 JUDE, servant true of Jesus Christ,
 of James the kindred seed,
to them by God the Father that
 are sanctified indeed,

2 And kept in Jesus Christ, and called,
 in patience to abide:
may mercy unto you, and peace,
 and love be multiplied.

3 When I, belov'd, gave diligence
 that I should unto you
of our salvation common write,
 'twas needful so to do,

4 Exhorting that ye earnestly
 should for the faith contend,
delivered once unto the saints
 to hold until the end.

Hymn 203
Jude 4-7

Old 18th

1 THERE certain 'mong you unawares
    crept in, which heretofore
  decreed were and ordained of old
    to condemnation sure;

2 Men godless and profane, which turn
    our God's grace from on high
  into unclean lasciviousness,
    and one Lord God deny;

3 And likewise our Lord Jesus Christ
    they also put to shame.
  Hence I to your remembrance bring,
    though once ye knew the same,

4 How that the Lord, once having saved
    his own from Egypt's land,
  thereafter them that disbelieved
    destroyed with mighty hand.

5 The angels also which kept not
    their proper first estate,
  but their own habitation left,
    hath he made desolate;

6 Reserved in everlasting chains,
    as under darkness bound,
  until the summons of the day
    of judgment great shall sound.

7 As Sodom and Gomorrha, with
     the cities of that place,
  together giving up themselves
     to fornication base,

8 And going after other flesh,
     are an example stern,
  the fiery vengeance suffering
     that endlessly doth burn.

Hymn 204
Jude 8, 11-13

Horsley

1 LIKEWISE these dreamers flesh defile,
     dominion they despise,
  whilst they against high dignities
     do evil speech devise.

2 Woe unto them! They Cain's way went,
     and Balaam's error held,
  and did with Korah perish when
     gainsaying he rebelled.

3 These spots are in your feasts of love,
     when feeding without fear
  and feasting with you: e'en as clouds
     that waterless appear,

4 Which carried are about of winds;
     trees withered in their fruits,
  quite fruitless, yea, twice dead are they,
     and plucked up by the roots;

5 Waves of the sea that rage and roar,
    and foam out their own shame;
  stars e'er reserved to darkness black,
    which wander without aim.

Hymn 205
Jude 14-16

Gerontius

1 AND Enoch also, seventh born
     from Adam, of these all
  in his own times in prophecy
    did to the people call:

2 Behold, the Lord doth surely come,
    and shall at last appear,
  ten thousands of his saints with him,
    in justice drawing near,

3 On all to pass due judgment, and
    convince each godless one
  'mong them of all their godless deeds
    which godless they have done,

4 And likewise of their speeches that
    with boldness forth they gave,
  which those that godless sinners are
    against him spoken have.

5 These, walking after their own lusts,
    both murmur and complain;
  their mouth doth speak great swelling words,
    which boasting are and vain,

6 Men's persons having all the while
   in admiration great,
to gain advantage of that which
   belongs to their estate.

Hymn 206
Jude 17-23

Redhead No. 66

1 DO ye, belov'd, recall the words
   which they aforetime spake
whom our Lord Jesus Christ himself
   did his apostles make;

2 How that they told you there should be
   men filled with mocking talk,
which after their own godless lusts
   should in the last time walk.

3 These be they which do separate,
   and always go astray:
of carnal mind and sensual,
   the Spirit have not they.

4 But ye, on your most holy faith
   yourselves upbuilding all,
and praying in the Holy Ghost,
   belov'd, these things recall;

5 As keeping in God's love, whilst ye
   look for the mercy sure
of our Lord Jesus Christ himself
   to life for evermore.

REVELATION

6 Do ye of some compassion have,
   when such to you appear,
so that ye make a difference:
   and others save with fear,

7 Them pulling forth out of the fire,
   whilst greatly hate do ye
the garment which hath by the flesh
   been spotted grievously.

HYMN 207
Jude 24-25
Palestrina

1 NOW unto him that able is
       your falling to prevent,
   and in his glory with great joy
       you faultless to present:

2 To God our Saviour, only wise,
       the glory let pertain
   with kingship, rule and pow'r, both now
       and evermore. Amen.

HYMN 208
Revelation 1:5-6, 8
Selma (short metre)

1 NOW unto him that hath
       his love on us bestowed,
   and washed us throughly from our sins
       in his own precious blood;

2 And made us to be kings
    and priests to him on high,
  brought faultlessly unto his God
    and to his Father nigh;

3 All glory be to him
    for ever to endure,
  and unto him dominion be,
    Amen, for evermore.

4 Behold, I Alpha am,
    and Omega, saith he;
  'tis I that the beginning am,
    and shall the ending be;

5 Saith he, which is and was,
    who is the Lord alone,
  yea, he which also is to come,
    and the Almighty one.

Hymn 209

Revelation 1:10-11, 19-20

Bangor

1 IN Patmos on the Lord's day I
      was in the Spirit found,
  and heard behind a mighty voice,
    as of a trumpet's sound:

2 I Alpha and Omega am,
    the first and last, said he:
  Write down, and to the churches send,
    the things revealed to thee.

3 Yea, write the things which thou hast seen,
        and likewise those things all
    which now occur, besides the things
        which be hereafter shall;

4 The myst'ry of the seven stars
        which in my right hand be,
    and seven golden candlesticks
        which are revealed to thee:

5 The seven churches severally
        have each their proper star:
    the seven candlesticks thou'st seen
        the seven churches are.

Hymn 210
Revelation 1:12-18

Ballerma

1 I, JOHN, did turn to see the voice
        that to me these things told.
    And turned, I seven candlesticks
        did see of purest gold;

2 And one like to the Son of man
        was 'midst the seven found;
    and he was with a garment clothed
        that reached unto the ground;

3 His girdle, all of gold, was made
        about the breasts secure.
    His head and hairs were white like wool,
        as white as snow most pure;

4 His eyes were as a flame of fire;
    like fine brass were his feet
as if within a furnace they
    did burn with fervent heat;

5 His voice as many waters was.
    In his right hand displayed
were seven stars; from his mouth went
    a sharp and two-edged blade;

6 His countenance shone as the sun
    that doth in strength excel.
And when I saw him, as one dead
    down at his feet I fell.

7 Upon me he his right hand laid
    as he did testify,
Arise, and be not thou afraid;
    the first and last am I:

8 Behold, I he that liveth am,
    and dead was; and, he saith,
I ever live, Amen; and have
    the keys of hell and death.

Hymn 211

Revelation 5:9-13

Lyngham

1 THOU worthy art, for thou wast slain,
    and thou hast by thy blood
from out of every kindred tribe
    redeemed us unto God,

REVELATION

2 From tongues and people, out of all
    the nations that there be:
  thou'st made us kings and priests to God,
    and reign on earth shall we.

3 Ten thousand times ten thousand, yea,
    and thousands thousands more:
  the voice of many angels sounds
    in praise for evermore:

4 Of pow'r and riches worthy is
    the Lamb that once was slain,
  all wisdom, glory, honour, strength,
    and blessing to obtain:

5 And every creature in the heaven,
    and earth, both near and far,
  and 'neath the same, and in the sea,
    and all that in them are,

6 Cried, Blessing, honour, glory, power,
    to him whom we adore
  upon the throne, and to the Lamb,
    Amen, for evermore.

Hymn 212

Revelation 7:9-10, 13-14

Argyle

1 A MULTITUDE whose number great
      no man could understand,
  from nations, kindreds, people, tongues,
    before the throne did stand;

2 And they in robes of white their place
    before the Lamb did take,
  and palms they in their hands did hold,
    and with a loud voice spake:

3 Salvation be unto our God
    which sitteth on the throne;
  and to the Lamb for evermore
    be praise and glory shown.

4 But who are these that are arrayed
    in robes of purest white?
  and whence came they unto the throne
    to dwell in glory bright?

5 These from great tribulation came
    to be in light arrayed,
  and in the Lamb's blood they their robes
    have washed, and white them made.

Hymn 213

Revelation 7:15-17

Orlington

1 WITH praise before the throne of God
    their voices always sound,
  and they shall serve him day and night
    within his temple found:

2 And he that sitteth on the throne
    among them shall remain:
  they shall not hunger any more,
    nor shall they thirst again.

REVELATION

3 The sun upon them shall not light,
    nor any heat at all:
  because the Lamb amidst the throne
    sustain and feed them shall;

4 And unto living waters' springs
    be led by him shall they:
  and God himself shall from their eyes
    wipe every tear away.

Hymn 214

Revelation 15:3-4

Effingham

1 THEY Moses' song, God's servant true,
    do sing both night and day,
  withal the song that hymns the Lamb,
    as with these words they say,

2 Lord God Almighty, all thy works
    both great and marv'llous be;
  thy ways are just, thou King of saints,
    and wrought in verity.

3 Who shall not be afraid, O Lord,
    and glorify thy name?
  because thou only holy art,
    as all thy works proclaim:

4 Before thee shall all nations come
    and worship in thy fear,
  for to the peoples of the earth
    thy judgments great appear.

Hymn 215

Revelation 19:11-16

Martyrs

1 THE heaven opened, and, behold,
 a white horse I did view,
and he that sat on him was called
 the Faithful and the True;

2 And he in righteousness doth judge,
 and goeth forth to war;
his eyes were as a flame of fire
 which burned with brightness pure;

3 And on his head were many crowns;
 and he did have a name
which written was, and none but he
 could understand the same.

4 And with a vesture he was clothed
 that had been dipped in blood:
and, lo, the name that he doth bear
 is called The Word of God.

5 And on white horses following
 were heaven's armies seen,
and they were in fine linen clothed
 that was both white and clean.

6 And forth out of his mouth doth go
 a sharp and burnished sword,
that with it he should swiftly smite
 the nations all abroad:

REVELATION

7 And he shall them in mighty power
    rule with an iron rod,
  and tread the winepress of fierce wrath
    sent from Almighty God.

8 And he both on his vesture hath
    and on his thigh the words
  that boldly written are, The KING
    OF KINGS, AND LORD OF LORDS.

HYMN 216

Revelation 21:1-4

Silchester (short metre)

1 I, JOHN, a heaven new
    and earth in vision saw:
  the heaven and the former earth
    had passed and were no more;

2 And there was no more sea.
    And, lo, behold did I
  the holy city, new and fair,
    Jerus'lem from on high,

3 Which down from God did come,
    from heaven far above,
  prepared as is a bride adorned
    meet for her husband's love.

4 And I from heaven heard
    a mighty angel tell,
  God's tabernacle is with men,
    and he with them shall dwell.

5 God with his people is,
    and be their God shall he.
  God from their eyes shall wipe all tears;
    and death no more shall be;

6 There shall no grief be there,
    nor crying, neither pain:
  the former things have passed, and shall
    no more be seen again.

Hymn 217

Revelation 21:5-7

Revive thy Work, O Lord + refrain
(short metre)

1 HE that sat on the throne
    said, All things make I new;
  and said he, Write thou: for these words
    both faithful are and true.

2 He said to me, 'Tis done,
    and all doth comprehend.
  I Alpha and Omega am:
    beginning and the end.

3 To him that is athirst,
    of water that doth live
  out of the springing fountain pure
    I plenteously will give.

4 He that doth overcome
    shall heir become of all:
  and I myself will be his God,
    and be my son he shall.

Hymn 218

from Revelation 21:10-23

There is a Fountain + refrain

1. UNTO a mountain great and high
   in spirit brought he me;
   and down from heaven, come from God,
   Jerus'lem I did see:

2. The city with God's glory shone
   and brightly did appear;
   her light was like a jasper stone,
   as precious crystal clear;

3. A wall she had, both great and high,
   and twelve gates therein set,
   and in them were those twelve tribes named
   which Isr'el did beget;

4. And twelve foundations had the wall
   about the city round,
   and of the Lamb's apostles twelve
   the names therein were found.

5. Foursquare the city lay, all fair:
   pure gold, like glass most clear;
   and in the wall's foundations there
   did precious stones appear.

6. Twelve pearls comprised the gates thereof,
   through which the people pass:
   the city's street was purest gold,
   like to transparent glass.

7 Throughout the city's length and breadth
    no temple did I see:
  for the Lord God Almighty and
    the Lamb the temple be.

8 The city neither of the sun
    nor of the moon had need:
  God's glory was the light thereof,
    the Lamb its light indeed.

Hymn 219

Revelation 22:12-13, 16-17, 20-21

Kedron

1 I QUICKLY come, saith he, and bring
    my sure reward with me:
  that I may give to every man
    as his own work shall be.

2 I Alpha and Omega am:
    beginning and the end;
  I am the first and am the last,
    and all things comprehend.

3 I, Jesus, have mine angel sent,
    that testify might he
  of those things in the churches which
    declared unto you be.

4 I David's root and offspring am,
    the bright and morning star.
  The Spirit and the bride say, Come,
    to all that hearers are.

REVELATION

5 Let him that hears say, Come. And let
   the thirsty come to me.
   And whosoever will let take
   of life the water free.

6 He which among you of these things
   true witness doth maintain,
   saith also, Surely unto you
   I quickly come. Amen.

7 Now even so, Lord Jesus, come,
   yea, quickly come again.
   The grace of our Lord Jesus Christ
   be with you all. Amen.

THE END OF THE HYMNS

Index of First Lines

	Hymn
A ministry more excellent	135
A multitude whose number great	212
Against the promises of God	60
All malice laying to one side,	173
Although we in the flesh do walk,	52
And Enoch also, seventh born	205
And these things unto you we write,	186
And this I pray, that yet your love	77
And we have seen, and unto you	195
And you, that sometime aliens	88
As each man hath received the gift	176
As having therefore boldness which	145
As in the body's unity	38
As loved and holy, God's elect,	93
As many as are of the law	58
As 'mong the people of old time	182
As Peter to the people spake,	4
As sin, and death by sin, the world	18
As touching righteousness of law,	81
At noon, said Paul, I in the way	9
Be therefore followers of God,	74
Before the judgment-seat of Christ	47
Behold, I unto you	41
Behold, not many wise men called	29
Behold, this is the covenant,	136

233

	Hymn
Belov'd, I wish above all things	200
Belov'd, ill follow not, but good.	201
Beloved, as ye always have	80
Beloved, be not ignorant	184
Beloved brethren, know ye all	171
But after we had suffered much,	96
But God forbid that I should boast,	64
But if of death the ministry	44
But in Christ Jesus ye who once	69
But we are bound to render thanks	101
By faith aforetime Abraham,	149
By faith did Moses parents cause	152
By faith the walls of Jericho	153
By faith, when Abraham was tried,	151
By no means let one you deceive	100
Christ being come a great high priest	139
Christ did not glorify himself	129
Christ suffered for us, and thereby	175
Consider him who patiently	155
Continue thou in those things which	114
Do not, my brethren well beloved,	161
Do thou remember that which I	111
Do ye, belov'd, recall the words	206
For Abraham believed in God,	57
For as we many members have	26
For both he that through sufferings	125
For Christ himself is entered not,	141
For of good things to come the law	142
For of the angels unto which	122
For they are not all Israel,	24
For this cause always thank we God,	97

	Hymn
For this cause faint we not, although	46
For when we yet were without strength,	17
From him that called you to Christ's grace,	55
From Peter, an apostle sent,	168
From Simon Peter, servant, and	179
Gird up your minds, be vigilant,	170
Go to now, ye that say, Today,	166
God hath us saved, and us by grace	110
God, who afore at sundry times	121
God's promise Abr'ham did believe,	15
God's servant, an apostle sent	117
God's wisdom and his knowledge rich	25
He antichrist is, that denies	191
He of the body, e'en the church,	87
He that sat on the throne	217
Herein our love is perfect made,	196
I, brethren, write no new command,	188
I, John, a heaven new	216
I, John, did turn to see the voice	210
I know that all of you, said Paul,	8
I, Paul, a preacher am ordained,	105
I Paul, as in mine absence long,	102
I Paul, in sufferings for you,	89
I Paul, the pris'ner of the Lord,	71
I quickly come, saith he, and bring	219
I render thanks unto my God,	120
I to my God on your behalf	28
I will endeavour to the last	181
I would not have you ignorant	98
If Abraham were justified	13
If one should suffer ill because	177

235

	Hymn
If then ye risen be with Christ,	91
If there among you any man	162
If ye fulfil the royal law	163
In Patmos on the Lord's day I	209
In scripture 'tis contained, Behold,	174
In that day when revealed shall be	10
Into the realm of his dear Son	86
It is impossible for those	130
Jude, servant true of Jesus Christ,	202
Keep this commandment without spot,	109
Lest I should tarry long, these things	106
Let all your conversation with	78
Likewise these dreamers flesh defile,	204
Love each the other one, for love	194
Mind ye the holy prophets' words,	183
Moreover, brethren, I would not	33
My brethren, as I follow Christ,	35
My brethren, be ye not deceived:	32
My brethren, with all diligence	180
My little children, let none you	192
My little children, that no more	187
No condemnation falls on them	21
No man the tongue can tame: it is	165
Not to the mount that might be touched,	157
Now, brethren, know ye not yourselves	31
Now, brethren, whatsoever things	83
Now in the Lord, and in his power,	76
Now, infants, it the last time is:	190
Now know we that whatever things	11

236

	Hymn
Now of the church Christ is the head,	75
Now say I, brethren, Let your walk	63
Now since we have this ministry	45
Now thanks be unto God in Christ,	42
Now therefore cast ye not away	147
Now therefore having been by faith	16
Now therefore unto you I write,	189
Now these all died in faith: not one	150
Now unto him that able is	207
Now unto him that hath	208
Now unto him that is of power	27
Now when the feast of Pentecost	3
Now when the law had been ordained,	138
O come ye out, be separate,	51
Of Abr'ham it is written that	62
Of our Lord Jesus Christ the God	65
Of our Lord Jesus Christ the God	169
Once and for ever sanctified	144
Paul, an apostle, (not of men,	54
Redemption have we through his blood,	66
See that ye one another love	172
Such an high priest became us, who	134
Take heed, lest there in any one	126
That cov'nant which was first decreed	137
That I might now be offered up,	116
That supplications, prayers, be made,	104
That we should one another love,	199
That which from the beginning was,	185
That which I of the Lord received	36

	Hymn
That whosoe'er is born of God	198
The armies of the aliens	154
The bodies of those beasts, whose blood	158
The cup of blessing, brethren, which	34
The earnest expectation of	22
The fellowship which doth pertain	70
The former treatise hath been made	1
The God of peace, that did again	159
The grace of God which unto us	118
The heaven opened, and, behold,	215
The heir, so long as him a child	61
The Lord hath sworn, nor will repent,	133
The love of Christ constraineth us,	48
The man that Moses' law despised	146
The same that did descend is he	72
The Spirit doth expressly speak	107
The things that unto man belong	30
The word preach, instant at all times,	115
Then, since we have a great high priest	128
There are diversities of gifts:	37
There certain 'mong you unawares	203
These things command and teach: let none	108
They Moses' song, God's servant true,	214
This faithful saying worthy is,	103
This know, that in the latter days,	112
This mind, which in Christ Jesus was,	79
This say I therefore in the Lord,	73
Thou hast my doctrine fully known,	113
Thou, Lord, in the beginning hast	123
Thou worthy art, for thou wast slain,	211
Though dead in trespasses and sins,	68
Though I with men's and angels' tongues	39
Through faith perceive we that the worlds	148
To Abraham, and to his seed,	14

	Hymn
To Abraham and to his seed	59
To one another own your faults,	167
To thank God, brethren, as is meet,	99
To you, and Isr'el all, be known	5
Today if ye will hear his voice,	127
Unto a mountain great and high	218
Unto one husband you I have	53
Upon him cast ye all your care,	178
Upon the church there came great fear,	6
We always unto God give thanks	94
We as the ministers of God	50
We have a consolation strong	132
We know that none is justified	56
We ought to give more earnest heed	124
We render unfeigned thanks to God,	84
We sometimes foolish were ourselves,	119
We then, as fellow-labourers,	49
What profit, brethren, doth appear,	164
What shall we say? Shall we in sin	20
What shall we say then to these things,	23
What then? So that grace might abound,	19
When, brethren, ye together meet,	40
When first Epaphras of your love	85
When God first unto Abraham	131
When he into the world doth come,	143
When Moses in the law had read	140
When ye into temptations great	160
Where then is boasting? If it be	12
Wherefore I also, after that	67
Who is he that shall of the world	197
With all men follow after peace,	156
With Peter the apostles stood,	7

	Hymn
With praise before the throne of God	213
With water truly John baptised,	2
Ye are complete in him, who is	90
Ye, little children, are of God,	193
Ye the epistle are of Christ	43
Your faith to Godward in each place	95
Your members therefore mortify	92
Your moderation in all things	82

Selected Verses for Singing

1 The following table has been compiled on the basis that no single hymn, or part of a hymn, should exceed eight verses.

2 With the great majority of the hymns there is no difficulty. Only a minority has more than eight verses, and of this number few are of any great length.

3 In the case of these longer hymns, great care has been taken to divide them into suitable parts, leaving the singer the choice of the selection presented. In many cases the hymn has fallen out naturally into two or more parts, as, for example, in Hymn 4 verses 1-6 or 7-12. In other cases the selection has been more difficult, in which case verses that do not occur in sequence have been combined to provide a suitable number in any one such hymn. An example of this can be seen in Hymn 181 verses 1-5 or, alternatively, 2-3, 6-9.

4 Although the selection of verses presented below has been arranged with great care, providing adequacy in the application of any given passage for singing, nevertheless it is to be stressed that

the singer must feel at liberty to select other verses which may be more suited to the occasion, in the worship of God through the singing of the hymns of the new testament.

Hymn	First Line	Verses

Acts

1	The former treatise hath been made	
2	With water truly John baptised,	
3	Now when the feast of Pentecost	
4	As Peter to the people spake,	1-6
	In the apostles' doctrine they	7-12
5	To you, and Isr'el all, be known	
6	Upon the church there came great fear,	
7	With Peter the apostles stood,	
8	I know that all of you, said Paul,	
9	At noon, said Paul, I in the way	

Romans

10	In that day when revealed shall be	
11	Now know we that whatever things	1-6
	But now the righteousness of God	4-5, 7-10
12	Where then is boasting? If it be	
13	If Abraham were justified	
14	To Abraham, and to his seed,	
15	God's promise Abr'ham did believe,	
16	Now therefore having been by faith	
17	For when we yet were without strength,	
18	As sin, and death by sin, the world	1-4
	But not as the offence, so is	3-8
	As therefore by the one offence	9-13
19	What then? So that grace might abound,	1-5
	For our old man is crucified	5-8
	For he, in that he died, died once,	8-12
20	What shall we say? Shall we in sin	1-6
	As to uncleanness servants then	7-12
21	No condemnation falls on them	1-6
	They that are of the flesh are all	6-11
	The body, if Christ in you be,	11-16
22	The earnest expectation of	1-3
	We of creation know that all	4-8
	For we by hope are saved: but hope,	7-11
	For good to them that do love God	12-15

Hymn	First Line	Verses
	(Romans)	
23	What shall we say then to these things,	1-6
	From the abiding love of Christ	6-7, 9-12
24	For they are not all Israel,	1-7
	What shall we say then? Is there found	8-13
	Nay but, O man, and who art thou	14-19
25	God's wisdom and his knowledge rich	
26	For as we many members have	
27	Now unto him that is of power	

I Corinthians

28	I to my God on your behalf	
29	Behold, not many wise men called	
30	The things that unto man belong	
31	Now, brethren, know ye not yourselves	
32	My brethren, be ye not deceived:	
33	Moreover, brethren, I would not	1-4, 10
		1, 4-9
34	The cup of blessing, brethren, which	
35	My brethren, as I follow Christ,	1-3
	Each man in prayer or prophecy,	4-7
	For covered never should a man	8-13
	How can it be a comely thing,	14-17
36	That which I of the Lord received	
37	There are diversities of gifts:	
38	As in the body's unity	1-4, 17-19
	For of itself no member can	4-9
	But now God in the body hath	8-15
39	Though I with men's and angels' tongues	
40	When, brethren, ye together meet,	
41	Behold, I unto you	

II Corinthians

42	Now thanks be unto God in Christ,	
43	Ye the epistle are of Christ	
44	But if of death the ministry	1-5
		1-2, 11-13
	Of that which was made glorious	4-10

Hymn	First Line	Verses
	(II Corinthians)	
45	Now since we have this ministry	1-6
46	For this cause faint we not, although	1-3, 7-9
47	Before the judgment-seat of Christ	
48	The love of Christ constraineth us,	1-4
	Moreover all things are of God,	5-10
49	We then, as fellow-labourers,	
50	We as the ministers of God	
51	O come ye out, be separate,	
52	Although we in the flesh do walk,	
53	Unto one husband you I have	

Galatians

Hymn	First Line	Verses
54	Paul, an apostle, (not of men,	
55	From him that called you to Christ's grace,	
56	We know that none is justified	
57	For Abraham believed in God,	
58	As many as are of the law	
59	To Abraham and to his seed	
60	Against the promises of God	
61	The heir, so long as him a child	
62	Of Abr'ham it is written that	1-5
63	Now say I, brethren, Let your walk	1-2, 6-10
64	But God forbid that I should boast,	

Ephesians

Hymn	First Line	Verses
65	Of our Lord Jesus Christ the God	
66	Redemption have we through his blood,	1-4
	For in him an inheritance	5-10
67	Wherefore I also, after that	1-2, 5-10
	The God of our Lord Jesus Christ,	3-8
68	Though dead in trespasses and sins,	1-4, 9
69	But in Christ Jesus ye who once	1, 5-9
70	The fellowship which doth pertain	1-4
	And for this cause I bow my knees,	5-10

Hymn	First Line	Verses
	(Ephesians)	
	Now unto him that is of power	11-12
71	I Paul, the pris'ner of the Lord,	
72	The same that did descend is he	1-6
		1-2, 7-8
		1, 7, 9-12
73	This say I therefore in the Lord,	
74	Be therefore followers of God,	
75	Now of the church Christ is the head,	
76	Now in the Lord, and in his power,	

Philippians

77	And this I pray, that yet your love	
78	Let all your conversation with	
79	This mind, which in Christ Jesus was,	
80	Beloved, as ye always have	
81	As touching righteousness of law,	
82	Your moderation in all things	
83	Now, brethren, whatsoever things	

Colossians

84	We render unfeigned thanks to God,	
85	When first Epaphras of your love	
86	Into the realm of his dear Son	
87	He of the body, e'en the church,	
88	And you, that sometime aliens	
89	I Paul, in sufferings for you,	
90	Ye are complete in him, who is	
91	If then ye risen be with Christ,	
92	Your members therefore mortify	
93	As loved and holy, God's elect,	

I Thessalonians

94	We always unto God give thanks	
95	Your faith to Godward in each place	
96	But after we had suffered much,	
97	For this cause always thank we God,	
98	I would not have you ignorant	

246

Hymn	First Line	Verses
	II Thessalonians	
99	To thank God, brethren, as is meet,	
100	By no means let one you deceive	1-4
	Already of iniquity	5-10
101	But we are bound to render thanks	
	I Timothy	
102	I Paul, as in mine absence long,	1-4
		1, 5-10
103	This faithful saying worthy is,	
104	That supplications, prayers, be made,	
105	I, Paul, a preacher am ordained,	1-5
	In silence let the woman learn	6-9
106	Lest I should tarry long, these things	
107	The Spirit doth expressly speak	
108	These things command and teach: let none	
109	Keep this commandment without spot,	
	II Timothy	
110	God hath us saved, and us by grace	
111	Do thou remember that which I	
112	This know, that in the latter days,	
113	Thou hast my doctrine fully known,	
114	Continue thou in those things which	
115	The word preach, instant at all times,	
116	That I might now be offered up,	
	Titus	
117	God's servant, an apostle sent	
118	The grace of God which unto us	
119	We sometimes foolish were ourselves,	
	Philemon	
120	I render thanks unto my God,	
	Hebrews	
121	God, who afore at sundry times	
122	For of the angels unto which	

Hymn	First Line	Verses

(Hebrews)

123	Thou, Lord, in the beginning hast	
124	We ought to give more earnest heed	
125	For both he that through sufferings	
126	Take heed, lest there in any one	
127	Today if ye will hear his voice,	
128	Then, since we have a great high priest	
129	Christ did not glorify himself	
130	It is impossible for those	
131	When God first unto Abraham	
132	We have a consolation strong	
133	The Lord hath sworn, nor will repent,	
134	Such an high priest became us, who	
135	A ministry more excellent	
136	Behold, this is the covenant,	
137	That cov'nant which was first decreed	
138	Now when the law had been ordained,	
139	Christ being come a great high priest	
140	When Moses in the law had read	
141	For Christ himself is entered not,	
142	For of good things to come the law	
143	When he into the world doth come,	
144	Once and for ever sanctified	
145	As having therefore boldness which	
146	The man that Moses' law despised	
147	Now therefore cast ye not away	
148	Through faith perceive we that the worlds	
149	By faith aforetime Abraham,	
150	Now these all died in faith: not one	
151	By faith, when Abraham was tried,	
152	By faith did Moses' parents cause	
153	By faith the walls of Jericho	
154	The armies of the aliens	
155	Consider him who patiently	
156	With all men follow after peace,	
157	Not to the mount that might be touched,	1-5
	But ye are to mount Sion come	5-11

248

Hymn	First Line	Verses

(Hebrews)

158 The bodies of those beasts, whose blood
159 The God of peace, that did again

James

160 When ye into temptations great
161 Do not, my brethren well beloved,
162 If there among you any man
163 If ye fulfil the royal law
164 What profit, brethren, doth appear,
165 No man the tongue can tame: it is
166 Go to now, ye that say, Today,
167 To one another own your faults,

I Peter

168 From Peter, an apostle sent,
169 Of our Lord Jesus Christ the God
170 Gird up your minds, be vigilant,
171 Beloved brethren, know ye all
172 See that ye one another love
173 All malice laying to one side,
174 In scripture 'tis contained, Behold,
175 Christ suffered for us, and thereby
176 As each man hath received the gift
177 If one should suffer ill because
178 Upon him cast ye all your care,

II Peter

179 From Simon Peter, servant, and
180 My brethren, with all diligence
181 I will endeavour to the last   1-5
    We cunning fables followed not   2-3, 6-9
182 As 'mong the people of old time
183 Mind ye the holy prophets' words,
184 Beloved, be not ignorant   1-4, 9-10
    For as a thief comes in the night   4-9

249

Hymn	First Line	Verses

I John

185	That which from the beginning was,	
186	And these things unto you we write,	
187	My little children, that no more	
188	I, brethren, write no new command,	
189	Now therefore unto you I write,	
190	Now, infants, it the last time is:	
191	He antichrist is, that denies	
192	My little children, let none you	
193	Ye, little children, are of God,	
194	Love each the other one, for love	
195	And we have seen, and unto you	
196	Herein our love is perfect made,	
197	Who is he that shall of the world	1-4
	If we men's witness do receive,	5-10
198	That whosoe'er is born of God	

II John

199	That we should one another love,	

III John

200	Belov'd, I wish above all things	
201	Belov'd, ill follow not, but good.	

Jude

202	Jude, servant true of Jesus Christ,	
203	There certain 'mong you unawares	
204	Likewise these dreamers flesh defile,	
205	And Enoch also, seventh born	
206	Do ye, belov'd, recall the words	
207	Now unto him that able is	

Revelation

208	Now unto him that hath	
209	In Patmos on the Lord's day I	
210	I, John, did turn to see the voice	
211	Thou worthy art, for thou wast slain,	
212	A multitude whose number great	

Hymn	First Line	Verses
	(Revelation)	
213	With praise before the throne of God	
214	They Moses' song, God's servant true,	
215	The heaven opened, and, behold,	
216	I, John, a heaven new	
217	He that sat on the throne	
218	Unto a mountain great and high	
219	I quickly come, saith he, and bring	

N.B. *Where the space allowed under the heading 'verses' is left blank in the table above, the whole hymn is to be sung.*

Textual Index

Text		Hymn
Acts		
1 : 1-4	...	1
: 5, 8-11	...	2
2 : 1-4, (6, 11, 14) 16-17	...	3
: 37-47	...	4
4 : 10-13	...	5
5 : 11-16	...	6
: 29-33	...	7
20 : 25-31	...	8
26 : 13-18	...	9
Romans		
2 : 5-9	...	10
3 : 19-26	...	11
: 27-31	...	12
4 : 2-8	...	13
: 13-16	...	14
: 20-25	...	15

Text	Hymn
(Romans)	
5 : 1-5	16
: 6, 8-10	17
: 12, 14-21	18
6 : 1-13, 14	19
: 15-23	20
8 : 1-14	21
: 19-30	22
: 31-39	23
9 : 6-24	24
11 : 33-36	25
12 : 4-8	26
16 : 25-27	27

I Corinthians

Text	Hymn
1 : 4-9	28
: 26-31	29
2 : 11-14	30
3 : 16-20	31
6 : 9-11	32
10 : 1-12	33
: 16-17	34
11 : 1-15	35
: 23-26	36

Text		Hymn

(I Corinthians)

12	: 4-11	...		37
	: 12-28	...	...	38
13	: 1-8	...	...	39
14	: 26-31	...	...	40
15	: 51-57	...	...	41

II Corinthians

2	: 14-17			42
3	: 3-6			43
	: 7-18	...	...	44
4	: 1-6	...	...	45
	: 16-18	...	...	46
5	: 10-11	...	...	47
	: 14-21	...	...	48
6	: 1-2	...	...	49
	: 4-10	...	...	50
	: 17 - 7 : 1	...	...	51
10	: 3-5	...	...	52
11	: 2-4, 13-15	...	...	53

Galatians

1	: 1-5	...	...	54
	: 6-12	...	...	55

Text			Hymn
(Galatians)			
2 : 16, 18-21	...	...	56
3 : 6-9	...	...	57
: 10-13	...	...	58
: 16-19	...	...	59
: 21-23	...	...	60
4 : 1-7	...	...	61
: 22-31	...	...	62
5 : 16-18, 22-25	...	...	63
6 : 14-16	...	...	64

Ephesians

1 : 3-6	...	...	65
: 7-14	...	...	66
: 15-23	...	...	67
2 : 1-9	...	...	68
: 13, 16-22	...	...	69
3 : 9, 11-21	...	...	70
4 : 1-6	...	...	71
: 10-16	...	...	72
: 17-24	...	...	73
5 : 1-5	...	...	74
: 23, 25-27	...	...	75
6 : 10-11, 13-17	...	...	76

Text	Hymn
Philippians	
1 : 9-11	77
: 27-30	78
2 : 5-11	79
: 12-16	80
3 : 6-11	81
4 : 5-7	82
: 8	83
Colossians	
1 : 3-8	84
: 9-13	85
: 13-17	86
: 18-20	87
: 21-23	88
: 24-29	89
2 : 10-15	90
3 : 1-4	91
: 5-11	92
: 12-17	93
I Thessalonians	
1 : 2-8	94
: 8-10	95

Text		Hymn
(I Thessalonians)		
2 : 2-5	...	96
: 13-16	...	97
4 : 13-17	...	98

II Thessalonians

1 : 3-10	...	99
2 : 3-4, 6-12	...	100
: 13-17	...	101

I Timothy

1 : (1-3) 4-11	...	102
: 15-17	...	103
2 : 1-6	...	104
: 7-15	...	105
3 : 14-16	...	106
4 : 1-6	...	107
: 11-16	...	108
6 : 14-16	...	109

II Timothy

1 : 9-11	...	110
2 : 8-15	...	111
3 : 1-6, 8-9	...	112
: 10-13	...	113

Text		Hymn
(II Timothy)		
(3) : 14-17	...	... 114
4 : 2-5	...	... 115
: 6-8	...	... 116

Titus

1 : 1-4	...	... 117
2 : 11-15	...	... 118
3 : 3-7	...	... 119

Philemon

: 4-7, 25	...	... 120

Hebrews

1 : 1-3	...	... 121
: 5-9	...	... 122
: 10-14	...	... 123
2 : 1-4	...	... 124
: 11-15	...	... 125
3 : 12-19	...	... 126
4 : 7, 9-13	...	... 127
: 14-16	...	... 128
5 : 5-10	...	... 129
6 : 4-9	...	... 130

Text		Hymn
(Hebrews)		
(6) : 13-18	... ...	131
: 18-20	... ...	132
7 : 21-25	... ...	133
: 26 - 8 : 3	... ...	134
8 : 6-9	... ...	135
: 10-13	... ...	136
9 : 1-5	... ...	137
: 6-10	... ...	138
: 11-12	... ...	139
: 19-23	... ...	140
: 24-28	... ...	141
10 : 1-4	... ...	142
: 5-9	... ...	143
: 10-13	... ...	144
: 19-23	... ...	145
: 28-30	... ...	146
: 35-39	... ...	147
11 : 3-7	... ...	148
: 8-12	... ...	149
: 13-16	... ...	150
: 17-22	... ...	151
: 23-29	... ...	152

Text		Hymn

(Hebrews)

(11)	: 30-34	...	...	153
	: 34-40	...	...	154
12	: 3-8	...	...	155
	: 14-17	...	...	156
	: 18-25	...	...	157
13	: 11-14	...	...	158
	: 20-21	...	...	159

James

1	: 2-6	...	...	160
	: 16-21	...	...	161
	: 26-27	...	...	162
2	: 8-13	...	...	163
	: 14-20	...	...	164
3	: 8-12	...	...	165
4	: 13-17	...	...	166
5	: 16-20	...	...	167

I Peter

1	: 1-2	...	...	168
	: 3-8	...	...	169
	: 13-17	...	...	170
	: 18-21	...	...	171

Text		Hymn

(I Peter)

(1) : 22-25	... ...	172
2 : 1-5	... ...	173
: 6-10	... ...	174
: 21-25	... ...	175
4 : 10-11	... ...	176
: 16-19	... ...	177
5 : 7-11	... ...	178

II Peter

1 : 1-4	... ...	179
: 5-10	... ...	180
: 15-21	... ...	181
2 : 1-3	... ...	182
3 : 2-7	... ...	183
: 8-14	... ...	184

I John

1 : 1-3	... ...	185
: 4-10	... ...	186
2 : 1-6	... ...	187
: 7-11	... ...	188
: 12-17	... ...	189
: 18-22	... ...	190

Text			Hymn
(I John)			
(2) : 22-29	...	...	191
3 : 7-11	...	...	192
4 : 4-6	...	...	193
: 7-13	...	...	194
: 14-16	...	...	195
: 17-21	...	...	196
5 : 5-13	...	...	197
: 18-21	...	...	198

II John

: 6-11	...	...	199

III John

: 2-8	...	...	200
: 11-12, 14	...	...	201

Jude

: 1-3	...	...	202
: 4-7	...	...	203
: 8, 11-13	...	...	204
: 14-16	...	...	205
: 17-23	...	...	206
: 24-25	...	...	207

Text			Hymn
Revelation			
1 : 5-6, 8	...	...	208
: 10-11, 19-20	...	...	209
: 12-18	...	...	210
5 : 9-13	...	...	211
7 : 9-10, 13-14	...	...	212
: 15-17	...	...	213
15 : 3-4	...	...	214
19 : 11-16	...	...	215
21 : 1-4	...	...	216
: 5-7	...	...	217
: 10-23	...	...	218
22 : 12-13, 16-17, 20-21	...	...	219

Sources of Recommended Tunes

1 The tune named at the head of each hymn is recommended for use with that hymn. The tunes have been chosen with great care and are mostly traditional psalm tunes, though some other tunes have also been included.

2 No tune has been used more than twice throughout the hymns, and a few tunes occur only once. Rarely, therefore, should two hymns with an identical tune be chosen in one and the same meeting. However, should this occur, the discretion of the precentor must be exercised as to the selection of an alternative tune.

3 With the exception of the common metre tune Grafton, all the suggested tunes may be found in the following books:

> The Methodist Hymn Book (35th Edition 1972)
> Hymns of Faith (1964)
> The Church Hymnary (April 1927)
> Companion Tune Book (6th Edition) to Gadsby's Hymn Book
> Second Supplement to Companion Tune Book (1974)
> The Scottish Psalmody (Free Church of Scotland) (sol-fa Edition 1977)
> Hymns for Today's Church (1st Edition 1982)
> Christian Hymns (1st Edition 1977) (Evangelical Movement of Wales)
> Sacred Songs and Solos (Sankey's) (1200 tune edition)
> The Scottish Psalter (1929) (staff edition)

4 In some cases an identical tune may appear under a different name in another tune-book: where this occurs, the alternative name is given in brackets in the following table. Again, different books render the same basic tune in varying forms: in that case we have referred to the

form of the tune considered to be most appropriate for the singing of the hymns of the new testament.

5 Unless indicated in the following table as short metre (SM), double common metre (DCM) or double short metre (DSM), all the tunes are straightforward common metre, with the exception of those few tunes which have repeating lines. For instance, with Repton, although basically a common metre tune, both the third and fourth lines are repeated in each verse.

Name of Tune	Source of Tune	No.
Abbey	Methodist Hymn Book (35th Ed. 1972)	698
Abney	Hymns of Faith (1964)	184
Amazing Grace	Hymns of Faith (1964)	50 (i)
Argyle	The Scottish Psalmody (Free Church of Scotland) (sol-fa Ed. 1977)	22
Arnold (Arnold's)	Companion Tune Book (6th Ed.)	91

★

Ballerma	Methodist Hymn Book (35th Ed. 1972)	559
Bangor	The Church Hymnary (April 1927)	313 (i)
Barrow	The Scottish Psalmody (Free Church of Scotland) (sol-fa Ed. 1977)	30
Beatitudo	Methodist Hymn Book (35th Ed. 1972)	604 (ii)
Bedford	Methodist Hymn Book (35th Ed. 1972)	155
Belmont	Methodist Hymn Book (35th Ed. 1972)	766
Bishopthorpe	Methodist Hymn Book (35th Ed. 1972)	107
Bristol	Methodist Hymn Book (35th Ed. 1972)	82
Brother James' Air	Hymns for Today's Church (1st Ed. 1982)	591 (ii)

★

Caithness	The Church Hymnary (April 1927)	481 (i)
Caroline	The Scottish Psalter (1929) (staff edition)	38
Colchester	The Church Hymnary (April 1927) Supplement	732
Coleshill	Methodist Hymn Book (35th Ed. 1972)	464
Covenanters (Covenanters' Tune)	Methodist Hymn Book (35th Ed. 1972) Additional Tunes	(AT) 5
Crediton	Methodist Hymn Book (35th Ed. 1972)	565
Crimond	Companion Tune Book (6th Ed.) Supplement	851

Name of Tune	Source of Tune	No.
Culross	The Church Hymnary (April 1927)	353 (i)
Dalehurst	Hymns of Faith (1964)	121 (i)
Denfield	Companion Tune Book (6th Ed.)	127
Drumclog	The Scottish Psalter (1929) (staff edition)	49
Duke's Tune	The Scottish Psalter (1929) (staff edition)	50
Dundee (Windsor)	Methodist Hymn Book (35th Ed. 1972)	237
Dunfermline	Methodist Hymn Book (35th Ed. 1972)	37
Effingham	Second Supplement to Companion Tune Book (1974)	923
Elgin	The Church Hymnary (April 1927)	246 (i)
Ellacombe (DCM)	Companion Tune Book (6th Ed.)	267
Evan	Hymns of Faith (1964)	261
Evangel (DCM)	The Church Hymnary (April 1927)	42
Forest Green (DCM)	Methodist Hymn Book (35th Ed. 1972)	897
French (Dundee)	Methodist Hymn Book (35th Ed. 1972)	625
Gerontius	Methodist Hymn Book (35th Ed. 1972)	74
Glasgow	Methodist Hymn Book (35th Ed. 1972)	904
Gloucester	The Church Hymnary (April 1927)	223 (ii)
Gräfenberg	The Scottish Psalmody (Free Church of Scotland) (sol-fa Ed. 1977)	70
Grafton	(source unknown) (American composer: Lowell Mason, Mus.D.)	

268

Name of Tune	Source of Tune	No.
Harington	Methodist Hymn Book (35th Ed. 1972)	413
Hebdomadal	The Church Hymnary (April 1927)	175
Hermon	The Scottish Psalmody (Free Church of Scotland) (sol-fa Ed. 1977)	74
Horsley	Methodist Hymn Book (35th Ed. 1972)	180

★

Invocation (DCM)	The Church Hymnary (April 1927) Supplement	746 (i)
Irish	Methodist Hymn Book (35th Ed. 1972)	503

★

Jackson (Byzantium) (Jackson's)	Methodist Hymn Book (35th Ed. 1972)	342

★

Kedron	Christian Hymns (1st Ed. 1977)	368
Kilmarnock	Methodist Hymn Book (35th Ed. 1972)	50
Kilsyth	The Scottish Psalter (1929) (staff edition)	76
Kingsfold (DCM)	Methodist Hymn Book (35th Ed. 1972)	154 (i)

★

Lloyd	Methodist Hymn Book (35th Ed. 1972) Additional Tunes	(AT)29
London New (London)	Methodist Hymn Book (35th Ed. 1972)	224
Lydia	Methodist Hymn Book (35th Ed. 1972)	1 (ii)
Lyngham (Nativity)	Hymns of Faith (1964)	1 (ii)
Lynton	Methodist Hymn Book (35th Ed. 1972)	442

★

Martyrdom	Methodist Hymn Book (35th Ed. 1972)	201

Name of Tune	Source of Tune	No.
Martyrs (Old Martyrs)	The Church Hymnary (April 1927)	520
Moravia	The Church Hymnary (April 1927)	306
Morven	The Church Hymnary (April 1927) Supplement	770 (ii)

★

Name of Tune	Source of Tune	No.
Nativity	Methodist Hymn Book (35th Ed. 1972)	85
Nearer Home (DSM)	Methodist Hymn Book (35th Ed. 1972)	658
Newington (S. Stephen)	Methodist Hymn Book (35th Ed. 1972)	56
Noel (DCM)	Methodist Hymn Book (35th Ed. 1972)	130
None but Christ (None but Christ can Satisfy) (with refrain DCM)	The Church Hymnary (April 1927)	699

★

Name of Tune	Source of Tune	No.
Old 18th (DCM)	The Church Hymnary (April 1927)	586 (ii)
Old 22nd (DCM)	The Church Hymnary (April 1927)	486
Old 81st (DCM)	The Church Hymnary (April 1927)	355 (i)
Orlington	Companion Tune Book (6th Ed.)	203

★

Name of Tune	Source of Tune	No.
Palestrina	The Church Hymnary (April 1927) Supplement	773
Petersham (DCM)	The Church Hymnary (April 1927)	398
Psalm 107 (DCM)	The Church Hymnary (April 1927)	151

★

Name of Tune	Source of Tune	No.
Redhead No. 66 (Waveney)	Methodist Hymn Book (35th Ed. 1972)	160
Repton	Hymns of Faith (1964)	95 (ii)
Rest	Methodist Hymn Book (35th Ed. 1972) Additional Tunes	(AT)23

270

Name of Tune	Source of Tune	No.
Revive thy work, O Lord (with refrain DSM)	Methodist Hymn Book (35th Ed. 1972)	738
Richmond	Methodist Hymn Book (35th Ed. 1972)	1 (i)

★

Name of Tune	Source of Tune	No.
S. Agnes	Methodist Hymn Book (35th Ed. 1972)	289
S. Anne (Ann's)	Methodist Hymn Book (35th Ed. 1972)	878
S. Bernard	Methodist Hymn Book (35th Ed. 1972)	408
S. Columba (Erin)	Methodist Hymn Book (35th Ed. 1972)	51
S. David	Methodist Hymn Book (35th Ed. 1972)	721
S. Flavian	Methodist Hymn Book (35th Ed. 1972)	43
S. Frances	Methodist Hymn Book (35th Ed. 1972)	454
S. Fulbert	Methodist Hymn Book (35th Ed. 1972)	604 (i)
S. James	Methodist Hymn Book (35th Ed. 1972)	307
S. Kilda	The Church Hymnary (April 1927)	558 (i)
S. Magnus (Nottingham)	The Church Hymnary (April 1927)	131
S. Mary	Methodist Hymn Book (35th Ed. 1972)	175
S. Matthew (DCM)	Methodist Hymn Book (35th Ed. 1972)	824
S. Mirren	The Scottish Psalter (1929) (staff edition)	117
S. Peter	Methodist Hymn Book (35th Ed. 1972)	99
S. Stephen (Abridge)	Methodist Hymn Book (35th Ed. 1972)	519
Salzburg	The Church Hymnary (April 1927)	562 (i)
Sawley	Methodist Hymn Book (35th Ed. 1972) Additional Tunes	(AT) 9
Selma (SM)	Methodist Hymn Book (35th Ed. 1972)	54
Sheffield (Attercliffe)	Methodist Hymn Book (35th Ed. 1972)	333

Name of Tune	Source of Tune	No.
Silchester (SM)	Hymns of Faith (1964)	363
Spohr	The Church Hymnary (April 1927)	451 (i)
Stracathro	Methodist Hymn Book (35th Ed. 1972)	102
Stroudwater	The Church Hymnary (April 1927) Supplement	747 (i)

★

Tallis (Tallis' Ordinal)	Methodist Hymn Book (35th Ed. 1972)	304
There is a Fountain (with refrain DCM)	Sacred Songs and Solos	129
Tiverton	The Church Hymnary (April 1927)	57
Torwood	The Scottish Psalmody (Free Church of Scotland) (sol-fa Ed. 1977)	140

★

University	Methodist Hymn Book (35th Ed. 1972)	49

★

Vox Dilecti (DCM)	Methodist Hymn Book (35th Ed. 1972)	154 (ii)

★

Westminster	Methodist Hymn Book (35th Ed. 1972)	73
Wigtown	Methodist Hymn Book (35th Ed. 1972)	512
Wiltshire	The Church Hymnary (April 1927) Supplement	735
Winchester (Winchester Old)	Methodist Hymn Book (35th Ed. 1972)	129
Wondrous Love (with refrain DCM)	Methodist Hymn Book (35th Ed. 1972)	337

★

York	Methodist Hymn Book (35th Ed. 1972)	347